The
Success
Factor

MASTER THE SECRET
OF A WINNING MINDSET

JOHN LEACH

PREFACE

We all know more or less what we mean by success. Success looks attractive. Successful people are respected by their community. Successful people look fulfilled. Successful people are somehow better than everyone else. We want to be successful.

Success means very different things to each of us. And crucial to becoming successful is defining for ourselves what success actually looks like. We need to be honest and realistic here, otherwise we risk setting ourselves up to fail.

No matter how hard I try, for example, I am not good enough at football to ever become a professional footballer, so there is simply no point in defining my own success as becoming one. Success is not money, either; while is true that many successful people become wealthy, there are many wealthy people who are far from successful. Neither is success the same as happiness, though the two qualities are surely closely linked.

You will need to think long and hard about what success means for you, and this book is designed to help you with that process.

We're all happy when we're doing what we like. But it would seem that most of us spend our time doing just the opposite. Research shows that around three-quarters of people feel unfulfilled in their jobs, yet this is what they spend most of their time doing. Not surprisingly, therefore, 80% of people say they want more out of life.

But what if you could spend most of your time doing something you're passionate about and make it a success? Although the old adage says that you should never mix business with pleasure, why should you spend your life not enjoying the work you do? Shouldn't you at least have a shot at achieving a more fulfilling life?

If this all seems a little 'pie in the sky' for your liking, consider the more practical side of the argument, and the idea of pursuing your passion successfully may not seem as crazy as it first appears. If you're passionate about something, the chances are you know a lot about it, are probably very good at it and are likely to work harder at it than anything else. And these are not entirely bad foundations for success.

Of course, this is just the start, and there's a lot more you need to do to follow your passion and turn it into a success, as the 80% of entrepreneurs who start up and then fail within five years have discovered. Armed with the right tools, however, entrepreneurs could give themselves a great chance of making it into the 20% who are in for the long haul. Similar statistics apply to most other walks of life, too.

As I said earlier, we all want to be successful; yet most people aren't successful. Why not? What is it that makes some people succeed while others don't? It is one of the world's perennial, significant questions which government after government all around the world tries to address.

I believe that we can all be successful if we want to. I have analysed hundreds of successful people in a wide variety of different walks of life, looking at what made them succeed. And even though a successful footballer needs very different skills in very obvious ways from a successful actor, business executive or journalist, what is remarkable is that to succeed they all need a set of qualities which, together, set them apart from everyone else.

I call that set of qualities **The Success Factor**.

In this book I set out 10 steps you can take to give yourself The Success Factor. If you follow these steps, you will succeed. But don't get me wrong. This is no easy path, no quick fix to life's problems. To be successful in life there are no shortcuts. That is why success feels so rewarding – when you get there, you will know you've earned it.

People who aren't successful don't follow one or more of these steps. Success is made, not born. I am absolutely convinced about this. No matter who we are, what backgrounds we have, and what innate talent or ability we were born with, success is made and not born. I have seen countless highly talented people fail, and many ordinary people succeed. Success is about achieving goals given what you have. And success is relative – what I might define as successful might not mean success to you and vice versa.

The great news about this is that, whoever you are, you can be successful. And I believe that success is in fact a choice. You can choose success if you want to. It's up to you.

Success is really all down to your mindset, as this will control your actions and your dealings with others. The Success Factor will help you to develop this winning mentality, and explain how you can apply it at key stages of your journey to make sure you reach your ultimate destination. Without the right mindset, your journey will be a constant uphill struggle, and any barriers that will undoubtedly appear will be far more difficult to negotiate. Mentally preparing yourself for the hard road to success will help you to overcome anything that is thrown at you along the way.

The fact that you're reading this book indicates that you want to be successful. I won't wish you luck, as I've learned that the harder people work, the more lucky they become. It really is up to you.

John Leach

Contents

Step 1
Define your vision

To give yourself the best chance of success, you need to build your future on the strongest foundations possible. But this isn't about people, money or power (although, if used wisely, all three can help you on your journey to fulfilment), it's about you.

This is your mission and your destiny that you're taking control of, so more than anything you need a vision that will shine like a beacon over everything you do, driving you forward to realise your dream. It has to be your ultimate goal; something you've always wanted to do and somewhere you've yearned to be. The mere thought of it will push you onwards when the going gets tough, help you to overcome the biggest challenges and triumph in the face of adversity. And when you reach your destination, it will be something that will be worth all the time and effort you've put in along the way.

So, before you set off on your road to success, you need to know where you're going and have a plan of how to get there. In this chapter, you'll find out how to define your vision of success and map out your journey to making it a reality, so that you can venture out with real purpose, direction and the confidence that you have what it takes.

1.1

The passion principle

Think about your heroes – all the big achievers and best performers across the spectrum of business, sport and beyond. What do they all share in common? The answer is a single-minded passion for what they do. It's the ultimate success factor.

Accessing your passion will have a profound impact on achieving your goals, being fulfilled and living a happy life. It can enrich your relationships with your family and work colleagues and, in business, it can engage, motivate and inspire your team to deliver outstanding results. This is because if you tune into your real passion, you will discover a drive and energy – also probably a joy – which you're unlikely to have encountered before.

Following your passion won't be easy. To achieve success both personally and professionally will take real focus and hard work. But you will be urged along by the ultimate motivation – pursuing something you love, enjoy and believe in.

Channelled in the right way, your passion will inspire those around you. It will act as a magnet for others. Your enthusiasm and motivation will capture the imagination, hearts and minds of people who will provide vital support to you in your personal life and work with you to help you realise your professional dream.

When you embark on a new project, a career move, or maybe a desire to set up your own business, if you can harness your passion, and surround yourself with people who share it, you will be destined for success rather than mediocrity.

But don't take passion for granted. Like anything else in life, it can be lost. Another success factor is knowing when your passion is waning and addressing the problem, and either working to rediscover your drive or looking for it elsewhere. However, first and foremost, your initial step towards success is to tune in to your passion.

> "Nothing **great** in the world has been **accomplished** without **passion.**"
>
> *Georg Wilhelm Friedrich Hegel*

The Passion Test

You'll know that you're following your passion if you can answer 'yes' to the four 'F's below:

Fun You really enjoy what you do; it provides a buzz and is a constant motivator

Fame We're not talking international celebrity status here, but you are recognised for what you do and others appreciate the contribution you make

Fortune Of course, wealth is relative, but we all have lifestyle needs. Having these needs satisfied is your own personal fortune

Future There is a sustained long-term horizon for what you are doing

> "If I had to name a **driving** force in my life, I would name **passion** every time."
>
> *Anita Roddick*

1.2

What is success?

No matter how passionate you are about something, you won't find success through passion alone. You need a clear direction that will guide you towards what success looks and feels like to you. This requires careful thought.

To follow your passion successfully, you need to determine how you want to pursue it and what your ultimate destination is. It's about defining your vision of success and using it as a blueprint or roadmap for achieving your goals. This should apply to relationships as well as your career or business, as the former can lay a solid foundation for the latter.

Distilling what you want to achieve helps to focus your energies and actions in the right direction. It's the starting point of a journey towards personal and professional fulfilment – and knowing your destination is vital.

Once you've determined your true passion, set out your vision for success and established the direction to take to get there, you'll probably find that life has an amazing way of giving you what you want. That's because you'll be able to channel all your passion and energy towards a single goal, and with such determination and commitment, you'll be equipped with the tools to shape your own future – to mould circumstances, situations and events to your demands in order to get closer to what you have set out to achieve.

Developing a definitive vision of your future aspirations requires clarity of thought. So take time out to think it through and see beyond the day-to-day clutter that clouds all of our minds. This will give you a clear picture of where you want to be. Then, if you reflect on where you are now, the way forward should jump into focus.

Distilling your true aspirations

A clear vision can take time to crystallise, it involves allowing time for self exploration and discovery, and you will need to consider:

★ **What** things are **important** to you? Everything flows from personal intentions.

★ **Why** are they important?

★ **How** will you feel if you don't **achieve** them?

"Your vision of where or who you want to be is the greatest asset you have."

Paul Arden

Your vision is the route to success, because it:

★ Creates a sense of direction and meaning

★ Helps you understand with clarity the relationships important for success

★ Provides momentum for change when you feel you deserve more

★ Creates a sense of what is important in your life

★ Provides a foundation for focused activity

"Our vision controls the way we think and therefore the way we act. The vision we have for our jobs determines what we do and the opportunities that we see or don't see."

Charles G. Koch

1.3

Setting goals

Forming your vision of where you ultimately want to be in life is a major achievement and a big step on the way to successfully following your passion. But your final destination can seem so far away that it feels like more of a dream than reality. To make it more real and prevent the sheer scale of what you want to achieve becoming too daunting, you need to break down your journey into smaller goals. This provides a map to reaching your destination. In the short term, it also becomes a motivator for action, driving you forward.

The key to successfully setting your interim goals is to ensure that they are aligned with your vision by staying focused on what you want to achieve. Otherwise, you run the risk of ploughing your energy into activities that appear to be useful in the short term, but are actually not taking you any closer to your vision. And the more energy you focus on reaching your ultimate goal rather than wasting it on other activities, the quicker you'll realise your vision.

Hitting these interim goals will be a satisfying experience – and one that delivers a sense of fulfilment and meaning. However, the kind of goals you set will be crucial. You'll need to have a trade off between the traditional view of only setting goals that are realistic and achievable, to avoid becoming demoralised, while at the same time, making sure they are stretching and challenging. After all, achieving your vision will not be easy, so to get there as quickly as possible, you need to be pushing yourself close to the limit at every stage.

"People with **goals** succeed because they **know where they are going.** It's as simple as that."

Earl Nightingale

Align your goals with your vision

In setting your interim goals, you should make sure they are key to realising your vision and not about short-term success. So you need to consider:

★ Relevance – how aligned is the goal to what you want to achieve?
★ Ability – your goals should be challenging, but not impossible
★ Timescale – set a realistic schedule for achievement
★ Support – take into account who will help you achieve your aim, and the skills they will contribute
★ Reward – celebrating hitting your targets in the right way will drive you, and your team, forward to your next task

Most important of all is being committed to achieving your goals – commitment and intention are potent ingredients for success.

1.4

Sense of purpose

Your vision for success must be supported by a strong sense of purpose. Setting the right goals to reach your destination acts as the stepping stones to success, fuelled by your passion for your vision. But it is your sense of purpose that will drive you from goal to goal.

If your vision truly reflects your passion and what you want to get out of life, and you have aligned a series of goals to take you there, you should be instilled with a strong sense of purpose – with a will to succeed.

When your vision is underpinned by the foundation of purpose, it provides traction to what you want to achieve in your life and your career. This in turn delivers accelerated performance, moving you closer to your target.

Purposeful people display self-confidence, creating an energy that attracts likeminded people, situations and circumstances that help them achieve their vision.

You must take time out to reflect on your purpose. Extraordinary things can be achieved when we have a sense of purpose. So often we see individuals with outstanding talents – musical, academic or sporting – never realise their full potential. This is because they lack a sense of purpose. Perhaps their vision of where they want to be was not aligned with the direction in which their talents have taken them. Perhaps they have been following others' vision for them rather than their own.

On the other hand, people with average ability who have clarity of purpose can achieve outstanding results.

Having a point to prove

This sense of purpose is often derived from:

★ Wanting to change something that is unjust
★ A deep desire to solve a problem – social, business or community
★ Wanting to prove to the world that you can be successful
★ A need to be the best you can be
★ A belief that your life or career owes you more than you are getting

"The moment one definitely commits oneself, then providence moves too. All sorts of things occur to help one that would never otherwise have occurred. A whole stream of events issues from the decision, raising in one's favour all manner of unforeseen incidents and meetings and material assistance, which no man could have dreamed would have come his way."

Johann Wolfgang Von Goethe

1.5

Who shares your vision?

You need to get all the key factors of passion, vision, goals and purpose in place early on in your journey to success, because you are likely to encounter plenty of opposition from the start. These will be from people in your everyday life – colleagues, and even friends and family – who don't share your vision.

Perhaps they think it's too big a risk, or don't believe you stand a chance of succeeding, or are jealous that you've found your true calling. Whatever their reasons, you need to be strong enough to counter their objections and negativity, and not allow them to derail your journey at the outset.

However, there will also be people out there who admire you for your ambition and share your values. They can prove invaluable in your mission by offering support and key insight, as well as important connections that can help to accelerate your success.

The secret is carefully working out who you can trust to support and foster your vision, and who, no matter how well meaning, are likely to place barriers in your way. So it's vital that, early on, you ensure that you share your vision with the right people, who can act as a catalyst going forward – and beware of the vision assassins, particularly common in the workplace, who can throw you into free fall if you're not careful.

> "A **friend** is one before whom
> I may **think aloud**."
>
> *Ralf Waldo Emerson*

Qualities to look for in your advocates

Finding the **right people** – advocates and mentors – who share your vision at the early stages of your journey can be invaluable to accelerate you along your path to success, and should:

- ★ Share your values and **beliefs**

- ★ Be **trustworthy** and a reliable source of advice

- ★ Bring genuine added **value** and knowledge

- ★ Be **interested** in what you do

- ★ Have no ulterior **drivers** other than a genuine **interest** in your success

- ★ Offer constructive advice that **motivates**

- ★ Be **available** when needed

> "Good listeners, like precious
> **gems** are to be **treasured**."
>
> *Walter Anderson*

1.6

Creating alignment

You'll need to think up a strategy – an idea or project – to kick start your journey towards fulfilling your vision. Depending on your aims, this could be anything from applying for a new job or getting a community project off the ground, to gaining a qualification or setting up a small business.

This strategy may help you attain the first of your interim goals or carry you through a number of them on the way to achieving your vision. Whatever your plan is, it's vital that your first project is successful. Failure could seriously dent your ambition. So you need to take a step back from your vision and disengage your passion for a moment to consider the practicalities of what you're about to embark on.

This is not about being negative. It's about making sure you have the necessary elements in place to make the project a success before ploughing ahead. Your passion and purpose are vital, but you also need to think carefully about the tactics you plan to use. You will need to assess and manage the risks that will undoubtedly exist and strike a balance between bravery and recklessness, using your head as well as your heart, and making sure you have the necessary resources.

Approaching new ventures and projects with a kamikaze and gung ho mindset could result in disaster. Carefully considering how you launch your journey to ensure a successful start will be crucial in building self-confidence and creating a solid platform for the future. If you can assess the pros and cons of a project from an objective and dispassionate viewpoint, then you can be secure in the knowledge that you possess one of the qualities necessary for being successful.

Balancing heart, head and wallet

The holy trinity of success:

★ Heart

Being **passionate** about your vision is essential as it can help to give you the edge over others and drive you forward with **real sense of purpose**.

★ Head

Carefully thinking about what you are planning is key to **avoid recklessness**, which can tarnish your reputation, damage your health and harm others. So apply a **rational mindset** to what you are looking to achieve.

★ Wallet

Do you have the resources to start **realising your vision**? If there's a chance you could lose a lot of money and leave yourself in a serious financial mess, you're unlikely to be successful, so either rethink your plan or set about getting the **resources** together and reducing the risks involved.

"Just as your car runs more smoothly and requires less energy to go faster and farther when the wheels are in **perfect alignment**, you perform better when your thoughts, feelings, emotions, goals, and values are in **balance**."

Brian Tracy

1.7

Define your values

In an increasingly digital world where information and the media are at everyone's fingertips, reputation has become a growing factor in success. A tarnished reputation, whether spread across the world's media or simply within a specific community or business sector, can bring down an individual or a business. What's more, in the rush to become successful, it's often something that is forgotten until it's too late. This is why it's very important to manage your reputation from the start.

The best way to do this is to lay down a series of values early on that will determine how you deal with others, whether friends, family, colleagues or customers. To build a good reputation and maintain it, these values should be set in stone and never be compromised. They should be an ethical barometer for your actions and eschew fair play in everything you do.

Achieving success by any means, foul or fair, can always come back to haunt you, as well as leaving a hollow, empty feeling when you have realised your vision. The global economic crisis that resulted from unethical behaviours will have repercussions for generations. The short-term gains experienced by individuals in the financial world has resulted in serious mistrust of the institutions, along with an erosion of the moral fibre of society – individuals that enjoyed strong personal reputations overnight became the enemies of the nation. Similarly, athletes taking the fast track to success by using performance-enhancing drugs end up paying a heavy price personally and professionally.

Success should never involve you compromising your values and your most fundamental beliefs of what is right and wrong. Achieving success should be done in a way that breeds long-term sustainable growth and in no way leaves any third party feeling abused, hurt or humiliated. Your values are an internal policing mechanism that governs what you consider to be right and wrong. Doing the right things in whatever you do will always pay long-term dividends.

Beware the dark side

Make a list of the values important to you in your quest for success – and stick to them. When preparing the list, consider what values are important to you. A good starting point is: 'Do unto others what you would have them do unto you'.

"If we are to **go forward**, we must go back and rediscover those precious values - that all reality hinges on **moral foundations** and that all reality has spiritual control."

Martin Luther King, Jr.

Playing fair creates:
- ★ Friendship
- ★ Respect
- ★ Loyalty
- ★ Kudos
- ★ Trust
- ★ Commitment
- ★ Satisfaction
- ★ Security

Playing dirty results in:
- ★ Dislike
- ★ Fickleness
- ★ Disrespect
- ★ Outrage
- ★ Disloyalty
- ★ Loneliness
- ★ Insecurity
- ★ Unrest

What would you prefer?

"It's not hard to make **decisions** when you know what your **values** are."

Roy Disney

1.8

Changing your mindset

The journey to reaching your vision will involve a number of stages or interim goals – the key milestones that will be your targets along the way, providing a route to your dream. Each stage will represent a progression either personally or professionally – or both, depending on your vision. As your goals move on, so will the circumstances you find yourself in and the challenges you'll face. It's likely that decisions you have to make will become more demanding and the risks more acute. To handle this changing environment, you'll need to progress personally, shifting your mindset to a new level at each stage.

The critical steps in growing a business or embarking on a challenging new project will place pressure on the way you think – it will push you into new areas and possibly further than you have gone before. It's likely to stretch your abilities to the limit. So it's important to adapt your way of thinking to be able to cope with the new risks and challenges each new situations brings. Otherwise you will find yourself frozen like at rabbit in the headlights, unable to make the necessary decisions to take you forward.

Successful entrepreneurs, for example, will tell you that growing their companies tested their capabilities to the breaking point. How comfortable will you feel if you need to give a personal guarantee to secure bank funding, or learn new skills to support the growth of your business or personal project?

To prepare yourself for the climb ahead, it pays to work out the different challenges you'll face as you move from achieving one goal to embarking on the next, so that you can be mentally ready to deal with them. Viewing each goal as a step towards your vision will help you to define the mindset that you need to develop to negotiate each stage successfully, allowing you to move forward with focus and clarity of thought.

Build your own Mindset Staircase

By looking at where you are now, where you want to be and the key stages that will take you there, you can determine the different challenges you'll face along the way and the mindset you'll need to negotiate each one successfully.

"When you are through **changing**, you are through."

Bruce Barton

Planning the steps:

★ At the foot of the staircase is where you are now

★ At the top of the staircase is your **ultimate vision**

★ The intervening **steps** consist of the various interim goals you have set yourself to get you to where you **want to be**

"To create something **exceptional**, your mindset must be relentlessly focused on the smallest detail."

Giorgio Armani

Facing the challenges:

★ Think **carefully** about each stage or goal

★ **Consider** the different situations that each one presents

★ Define the **mindset** you'll need to raise yourself from one stage to the next

1.9

Grasp the opportunities

To avoid wasting critical time and energy in realising your vision, you will not only need to be vigilant for key opportunities that can speed you forwards, but also to act on them quickly and decisively when they arise.

This may seem straightforward, but it is likely to require a fundamental change in the way you currently behave. This is because most people have a tendency to take the easy option, put off making difficult decisions and shy away from taking risks. As a result, many people go through life regretting that they did not do certain things and take particular actions that could have meant that their lives turned out differently – perhaps more successfully and taking them closer to where they would have preferred to be.

Instilling yourself with the courage to make difficult decisions and take the necessary risks to ensure you seize key opportunities will play a vital role in achieving the success you crave.

We constantly reach crossroads in our day to day existence, and at these points we have to make a decision about which way to turn. Rather than taking the path of least resistance, you need to harness and focus your sense of purpose from your passion to succeed and make your choice based on which route will accelerate you towards your vision.

You need to understand the signals, spot the opportunities and go in with your mind open to the potential risks, so that you are ready to deal with them and seize your chance to get closer to your goal. That way you'll replace the 'if only's and 'what if's with the satisfaction that you grasped the moment and have no regrets.

Seizing the moment

There are many reasons and circumstances that could hold you back from capturing the once-in-a-lifetime opportunities that could help you realise your vision:

★ **Fear** of humiliation

★ Family **commitments**

★ Financial **risk**

★ Personal **insecurity**

"Life's race well run, life's work well done."
Grave inscription, anonymous

To provide the additional motivation you may need, consider how doing so could increase your standing and status. Ask yourself the following questions, and think about how seizing the opportunity will make a difference to how you're viewed:

★ How do people **describe** me as a person?

★ What **contribution** do my peer group think I make?

★ What great things do people think I have **achieved**?

★ What **gaps** would I leave if I were no longer here?

★ What do I want to be **remembered** for?

1.10

Vision without action equals hallucination

Having taken the time to set out your vision, and mapped a route to achieving it, a real test of your commitment to following your passion is whether you are doing something about it or not.

Determining whether you're actually acting on pursuing your goals can be more difficult than you might think. Much of the work is, indeed, deciding on your true passion and defining a vision of where you want to take it. Then you need to form a sense of purpose, consider the challenges you'll face along the way and prepare yourself mentally for the journey.

But all this preparation will be in vain if you fail to take the first positive step towards your goal and then continue to drive yourself forward. What's more, it's important that you're not only progressing towards your mission, but that you retain the focus to make sure that you're moving in the right direction.

The risk is that you convince yourself that you are heading for your goals, but in fact have veered off course or are not actually moving at all – you are simply standing still instead.

The key is to constantly review your progress to make sure you're still heading in the right direction. This will mean that if you to stray from the path, you should be able to quickly get yourself back on course.

Be a Doer, not a Talker

People who pursue their vision with direct action are Doers, and they:

★ Speak with **confidence** and a ruthless simplicity

★ Are **consistent** with words and actions

★ Are **interesting** to listen to

★ Just get on with it

★ **Deliver** results

Conversely, individuals that claim to have strong goals, but don't really are Talkers, and they:

★ Constantly change their mind

★ Are consistently inconsistent

★ Are not taken seriously

★ Become sidelined by peers and are labelled as dreamers

★ Fail to deliver and make excuses

Make sure you're a Doer by constantly questioning your actions:

★ Have the goals you set been **achieved?**

★ Are you putting in the required **time** and **effort** to get to where you want to be?

★ What needs to change to make your vision a **reality?**

★ Are you genuinely pleased with your **progress?**

★ What do you need to **change?**

"There are no **gains** without pains."

Benjamin Franklin

purpose, focus, motivation, sanctuary, advice, vision, determination, clarity, support, commitment

Step 2
Prepare

You'd be crazy to run a marathon without preparing yourself in advance, both mentally and physically. Not doing so would give you little chance of success, and even if, by some miracle, you did manage to finish the race, you'd be well down the field and would certainly run the risk of doing yourself some serious harm in the process. The same goes for your quest to realise your vision.

You've found your passion, pinned down exactly what success means to you and set yourself a provisional series of goals to light your way. Now you need to get yourself in peak condition for the long road ahead. Although staying physically fit by taking regular exercise and eating healthily will help by keeping you mentally alert, energised and robust, it's arguably your head rather than your body that needs the most preparation.

This chapter focuses on how you should go about getting yourself in shape so that you can launch your mission on top form, brimming with purpose, vigour and mental strength to give yourself the best possible start and maximise your chance of hitting your key goals. Your mindset is crucial, along with making the right connections to help you stay mentally strong.

2.1

Building resolve

Life's full of ups and downs. The highs drive us forward, while the lows can drag us down. The key to successfully achieving your vision is to make the most of the impetus that the highs bring, but prepare yourself mentally for the lows, so that they don't sap your will to succeed.

Constantly being forced to explore alternative roads to our desired destination will be wearing and you may find yourself asking: "What's the point in doing this? Is it really worth it?"

At these critical points, it can be easier to give up than to carry on – but to be successful you will have to dig deep, maintain focus and continue with your mission, and accept that setbacks are just part of the game plan.

When you plan your interim goals to reach the summit of your vision, you will consider the challenges at each stage and plan to change your mindset accordingly. But there will also be unexpected challenges in between, and their cumulative effect will really test your resolve. If your vision is true and your passion strong, then you will be able to cope with the setbacks and return stronger and more determined to succeed.

If you really want it, you will have an insatiable desire and the will to succeed. Building this mental toughness is one of the most important ingredients for success. It is vital to condition your mind to becoming resilient. Without it, winning becomes more difficult.

So take strength from adversity. When it all seems too much, reflect calmly on why you're doing this. Remind yourself what you're striving for, that it was never going to be easy and that you have confidence in your own ability to succeed. After all, the harder the road, the greater the feeling of achievement at the end, and the sweeter the taste.

"If you're going through hell, **keep going**."

Winston Churchill

Rewind, accept and have faith

When things are not going your way, embrace the principles of RAF to get you through:

★ Rewind and go back to your vision, picture success and hold this image in your mind. Quiet contemplation is vital to aiding this process. This activity will move you out of the negative state and refresh your mind to get you back "on purpose".

★ Accept that things will not always go your way. Avoid long drawn out dissections of why things turned out the way they did. Coming runner up is sometimes a wake up call for us. Accept the position and move on otherwise negative self talk will hinder progression.

★ Have Faith in yourself and your ability to achieve what you want out of life. When you develop faith, bouncing back when things go wrong is far easier. By having faith you convince your mind that anything is possible.

Practice this philosophy and see your success improve dramatically.

"Difficulties **strengthen the mind**, as labour the body."

Seneca

2.2

Reflect and recharge

When you're focused on realising your vision, you're pursuing it with such purpose and commitment that it's easy to immerse yourself fully and forget that you need to take time out to reflect on your progress and strategy. You need to regularly pull yourself away from your day-to-day duties, so that you can review the work you've done and plan ahead. If you don't, you can end up losing direction and becoming less productive. Periods of reflection provide a sanctuary for the clarity of thought you need to make sure your mission is on track.

This practice of finding sanctuary helps to remove mental blockages and fosters a sense of balance between work and play. Without regular periods of reflection eventually you could find yourself in a rut – the place you don't want to be!

To make sure you take the necessary time out, plan three levels of sanctuary and embed them into your daily routine:

Level 1 – Daily sanctuary to help you prepare for the day ahead. Starting each day with 10 minutes of deep reflection provides a kick start to focused activity and awareness.

Level 2 – Weekly sanctuary that helps divert your energies into non-related activities, such as pursuing a hobby, sport or spending more time with family and friends. These activities offer an important diversion so you return to pursuing your vision refreshed.

Level 3 – Extended sanctuary includes those activities that most people can only fit in two or three times a year. They would typically involve family holidays; short breaks or some form of retreat. This gives you time not only to relax and recharge, but also to view the bigger picture, assess your progress and consider what needs to change going forward. Sometimes you just have to stop, look and listen to what is going on around you!

Planning your escape

Get into a routine of doing things that will help you to find sanctuary:

★ **Plan out your social life with family and friends** – try to get into a routine of meeting up with friends to stay connected to the real world

★ **List your favourite places** that you have not been to for a while, then draw up a schedule of when to visit them

★ **Go on a retreat** – this will help to quieten the mind and remove the noise associated with daily hectic living

★ **Join a gym and take more exercise** – this is a great way of clearing your mind and upping your energy levels

★ **Visit a place of historic significance** – then you're also occupying and expanding your mind while you relax

★ **Connect with nature** – visiting the countryside, the sea and mountains all get you into the healthy outdoors

Remember, there's no excuse for being too busy! You must live your life in a state of total awareness!

"Every now and then go away, have a little **relaxation**, for when you come back to your work your **judgment** will be surer. Go some distance away because then the work appears **smaller** and more of it can be taken in at a glance and a lack of **harmony** and **proportion** is more readily seen."

Leonardo Da Vinci

2.3

Dealing with loneliness

Successful people often talk about the feeling of isolation they experience when pursing their desired aims and objectives. In pursuit of your vision, you are likely to find yourself in the driving seat, making the big decisions and shouldering a lot of the responsibility. You may be the one in charge, or working on your own towards your goal: this can be a lonely place.

Striving for success invariably involves expeditions into the unknown, which will involve you making decisions that few people will have the experience to help you with, so it's vital that you can work under your own steam, motivate yourself and not give into the insecurities that this situation can bring. This is something you'll need to face up to and prepare yourself for, but equally you should reduce the feeling of isolation where possible by building your own support network of colleagues and confidantes to help you share the burden and contribute ideas.

With your constant focus on the end game and how to get past the finish line, it's easy to shut yourself off and think that only you alone are equipped to make the decisions to take your forward. But by withdrawing into yourself you can lose your grip on reality. Other people's input can broaden your perspective, throw up ideas you may never have thought of, reinforce your belief in yourself and your mission, help inform key decisions, motivate you and ultimately accelerate you towards your vision.

Yes, there will be times when no one can help you and you need to work in isolation, but you should never isolate yourself from those who can provide invaluable help.

Combating isolation

In the process of moving towards a successful and fulfilling life and career, you need to take some simple steps to combating loneliness:

★ **Smile** – Don't signal your loneliness to your peers and others you are trying to influence. This could have an adverse effect on how you are perceived.

★ **Talk to friends** – We all have friends outside of work so make sure you talk to them. They are a great source of support and advice.

★ **Learn** – New situations and environments will require new knowledge, the more you know the more confident you become and the less isolated you feel.

★ **Be friendly** – Be nice to everyone you meet, it makes people warm to you and you can feed off their energy.

★ **Attend events** – Networking events where like-minded people congregate provide an ideal opportunity to share experiences and war stories.

★ **Create ambassadors** – Build relationships with people that support your points of view. Ensure that you communicate with them and keep them in the loop of what you are thinking and doing – they become your advocates and your extended voice.

You may feel alone and isolated, but you must take comfort in the fact that at some point in their progression to success, others have felt exactly the same.

"Most of the **important things** in the world have been accomplished **by people** who have kept on **trying** when there seemed to be no hope at all."

Dale Carnegie

2.4

Connect to a community

In whatever arena you want to succeed, you'll benefit from identifying and ultimately joining a relevant community, where individuals with common interests share and connect with each other. By doing so you'll meet like-minded people whose experiences, thoughts and attitudes could make a big contribution to your own success.

The entrepreneurial world has seen a dramatic rise in the number of business networking groups, acting as a source of personal and business development. These groups encourage networking and interaction. Not only do they stimulate business activity, but they also act as a portal of real-life experiences that help you make tough decisions and face key challenges.

Beyond business, thanks to the internet and digital technology, there has been a growth in support groups and social networks that allow people to build relationships, and share problems and best practice. They range from facebook to more specific online groups that frequently organise events to allow their members to meet up face to face. They're great for encouraging individuals to channel their passion, they can prove motivational and help you to raise the bar.

Be an active member of your community network, and you're likely to be repaid several times over. Don't ignore the opportunities to connect and spread the word that facebook, Twitter and other social networking websites provide. They offer a great opportunity to broaden your connections and create advocates. Over time you can build a Golden Circle of Connectors – people whose opinions and inputs you both trust and respect, and who can help you to make things happen.

Building links with key communities will help you to move forward.

Get connected

Joining a relevant community and sharing experiences can provide invaluable help when:

★ Difficult decisions have to be made

★ You don't know how to address a particular challenge

★ You are unsure as to which direction to take

"Shared joy is a double joy; shared sorrow is half a sorrow."

Swedish Proverb

Your personal success will improve significantly when you get involved with your community of interest. It will give you the opportunity to:

★ Mix with individuals who have similar **aspirations**

★ Build **personal relationships** that can be vital to you in times of need

★ Share your **wisdom** and build kudos

★ Exchange contacts that offer **mutual benefit**

★ Create **expert** advocates and ambassadors

"I felt it shelter to speak to you."

Emily Dickinson

2.5

Learn from success

Get into the habit of finding out about successful people and how they have achieved their goals. You may simply be able to talk to them directly if you know them personally (family, friends, colleagues, boss), or you can research and read up about them. Their leadership style, their ability to motivate teams, how they overcame adversity and their account of their road to success can all prove to be inspiring nuggets that you can use to propel you towards your own vision.

You can use their experiences to guide your own life. Read their stories of hardship and how mental toughness helped them face major challenges. Carefully consider what you read and distil the key elements that are relevant to your situation, and then think about how you can learn from them.

Are you clear in your own mind who influences you? Whose achievements do you admire? Has anyone successfully achieved a vision similar to yours? Answering these critical questions can help you select the most relevant people to tap into. Then you can use their methods, techniques and insight to fast track your own success. Cherry picking people's knowledge can be extremely beneficial to your own situation. They can help you to change your behaviour and identify the skills you may lack.

Comparing your own performance and attitudes to those people you consider successful, then implementing a plan of action to embrace aspects of their approach can be a very powerful exercise.

Learning from others

To learn how you can learn from other people's success:

1. List those people that you aspire to, who have influenced the way you think or whose success you would like to emulate. This could be your boss, a colleague, and a high flyer in your organisation or a famous person.

2. Define very clearly what it is that makes them successful in your eyes, focusing on specific behaviours, skills and attitudes.

3. Make a list of the top 10 attributes that you believe would be beneficial if you integrated them into your own approach. Go through your list and score yourself on a scale of 1-10. How do you compare?

4. Highlight those areas where you think improvements need to be made. Initially, choose five things to work on and review their impact each month.

"Find someone whose hindsight can become your foresight."

Mahatma Gandhi

2.6

Monitor your thoughts

A key part of getting yourself in shape to successfully pursue your vision and building mental strength to drive you forward is training your mind towards positive thought. We all have many conversations with ourselves throughout the day in response to the situations we encounter. Keeping them positive will have the effect of flattening out the peaks and troughs in your moods. Because the way you handle situations will be directly influenced by your thoughts and mood, this approach will result in more positive outcomes.

With every challenge you face and every barrier you try to overcome, it's important to take away the positives rather than focusing on the negative aspects of the struggle. Sometimes it's easy to let your mind dwell on the problems as you relive the experiences in your mind, meaning the struggle may have been prolonged resulting in anxiety. It's important to learn from these situations, but dwelling too much on the fight rather than the positive outcome can hold you back. Sustained periods of failure or experiences that resulted in humiliation, anger, disappointment, fear, hurt or injury can trigger a whole series of negative inner discussions that can sabotage achieving your vision.

As part of your conditioning for success, it is vital that you listen carefully to and control the conversations you have with yourself, as they can have a powerful effect on how you act. Focusing your thoughts and internal conversations on the positive can act as a catalyst in helping you get what you want out of life.

> "We are what we think. All that we are arises with our thoughts. With our thoughts, we make the world."
>
> *Buddha*

Accentuate your positive thinking

Here are some simple steps to build into your daily routine to ensure you eliminate the negative thoughts that can stunt your personal growth and hinder progression towards your vision:

1. Take five minutes every morning to clear your mind of lingering negative thoughts and memories from the previous day. Tell yourself that today will be **better** – it gets you off to a good start.

2. Be constantly and consciously **aware** of what you are saying to yourself.

3. Stop judging everything you see as being right or wrong, just **accept** it for what it is – by doing this you use far less emotional energy.

4. Tear down the mental barriers to success by **eliminating** negative thoughts such as "I can't", and replacing them with "I can" or "I will".

> "With the new day comes new **strength** and new **thoughts**."
>
> *Eleanor Roosevelt*

2.7

Handling failure and rejection

Learning how to handle the tough times on the journey towards your vision when things don't go to plan can help to strengthen your mindset, reduce your negative thoughts and prevent your self-confidence and drive from suffering.

When you embark on following your passion, like the many successful people who've gone before you, you must accept from the outset that rejection and failure will feature on the route to ultimate achievement. Some days you will inevitably feel that the energy going into realising your vision is almost inversely proportional to success.

Entrepreneurs in the world of business will regularly talk about the constant rejection from customers. Consider the ambitious new graduate who sends their CV to numerous employers with constant feedback of: "Thanks, but no thanks." Success in the world of cinema and theatre has seen many a global star emerge from literally hundreds of failed auditions.

Rejection must be viewed as a temporary setback in our lives. You must avoid becoming disheartened by a negative result and view it as a learning experience – one that you can take something from and share with others.

It's natural to get annoyed with yourself and be hyper critical of your performance. Watch your favourite sports star the next time they fall short of the mark. You can see it written all over their face, or watch them giving themselves a good telling off. For them, rejection and failure acts as a wake-up call, pushing them to greater heights next time. Use negative situations to positive effect, as motivation to improve.

"Failure is success if we learn from it."

Malcolm S. Forbe

You can take simple steps to cope with rejection and transform a negative experience into a positive force:

★ Ask why – It is vital that you seek feedback as to why you were rejected or failed. Whatever the reason you must learn from the experience and take advice that will help the next time round. People are usually more than happy to offer constructive criticism. Finding out why you failed is often more useful than how you triumphed.

★ Don't take it personally – Rejection may simply come from the fact that it was not yet your time to succeed. Avoid wallowing in self pity and just appreciate the outcome. Avoid issues of pride as this will merely instigate negative thoughts.

★ Transiency – How important will your future be tomorrow? It's never as bad as it looks. Just ask yourself whether it will make a difference in 100 years' time. Move on!

★ One step closer to victory – Some people would say that it takes nine 'no's before you get a 'yes'. Remember, each rejection gets you one step closer to the acceptance.

★ Think back – You must focus on your purpose and vision. You know why you are doing it, so just keep on going. This should provide you with the necessary motivation to get back to the task in hand.

★ Action plan – Make a list of the things you need to get better at. Look dispassionately at what you are doing and how you are doing it. Think about what can be improved and then create an action plan to move you forward.

2.8

Look for energisers

There are two groups of people that you will come across in your quest to succeed – one, the energisers, will provide inspiration; the other, the sappers will drain you of energy and make you question your very being.

It is vital that your desire for success is only communicated to those with a genuine heart-felt interest in your success. Energisers should form the most significant part of your personal network. While they are positive in their outlook, they are also pragmatic and can view situations and opportunities with ruthless simplicity. They will tell you how they see it. However, this will be communicated with candour and respect, so be sure to associate with these individuals.

Energisers are the mental stimulants successful people need to keep them going. They will provide invaluable support to help you through tough times. Energy sappers, on the other hand, will eat away at your internal motivation and dreams.

Not only should you associate with energisers, but also you must become one yourself, because, in turn, you will attract others. This magnetic effect starts to create a group of people that think in the same way. With sufficient critical mass, these individuals become the catalyst for massive change in communities, economies, arts and politics.

The Impressionist movement in Paris, for example, in the early 1800s and the Motown record label in the 1950s both came about by groups of energisers – energetic individuals with a passion to do something big. Energisers spark off each other, they debate and enthuse. They are the pioneers and innovators who develop new possibilities that deliver groundbreaking ideas.

Energisers can change the world, make sure that you are surrounded by them!

Energisers and sappers

It's important to know the key characteristics of these groups of people as they can have a key influence on your success:

Energisers

★ View life as one big **opportunity**

★ Are motivated individuals who set ambitious goals and look for the next big thing

★ Have positive outlook built on clarity of thought and a desire to make a difference

★ Are warm and **welcoming** and refrain from judging

★ Create a positive environment out of a sense to do well

★ Can make the unthinkable a **reality**

Sappers

★ View life as one big problem

★ Have no sense of personal clarity

★ Are quick to judge

★ Envy other people's success and can be organisational saboteurs

★ Can suppress the desires and motivations of ambitious people

★ Create an unhealthy atmosphere through their negativity

"Whether they burst with **excitement** or simmer quietly, when you're in the presence of enthusiastic people, you feel happier and more excited about your life, perhaps you even feel **inspired**."

Mary Marcdant

2.9

Control the things you can

Your focus on becoming a success should be so strong that you want to influence or control everything that may have an impact on it. As a result, generally, your destiny can largely be guided by your thoughts, actions and behaviours. However, there will always also be external factors at play that you can't control, which could have an impact on your ambitions. These could vary from environmental factors, through to political and social issues, as well as the behaviour and actions of other people.

However, success comes from managing the factors you can control, not those you can't. Embracing this principle will get you motivated to move forward on those pressing issues that need dealing with. Focusing on factors outside your sphere of influence can create unnecessary stress and reduce the effectiveness of your actions.

Worrying about things you have no influence over can become a dangerous preoccupation, as it will take you no closer to your goal, and will simply waste valuable time you could be dedicating to doing this. What's more, your mental strength can be eroded by the enormity of the task associated with dwelling on the things you can't change. Focusing on those you can is the only way forward, while being ready to deal with the unexpected, should the situation arise.

When you master the art of controlling the controllable, you'll be directing all your available energy towards success, and will gain a better balance between activity and thinking.

Know your sphere of influence

Don't waste time on factors out of your control. Instead, focus on the 10 things you can:

1. **Attitude** – believe you can make your dreams come true

2. **Learning and knowledge** – you must learn and acquire knowledge if you want success

3. **Friends** – who you spend time with and who you share ideas with

4. **Motivation** – the invisible force that comes from within

5. **Time** – how you spend your time; who, with, and on what

6. **Capabilities** – what you are providing to others and how effectively you deliver it

7. **Financial matters** – what you spend and your means

8. **Interaction with people** – always with respect, honesty and integrity

9. **Impact on the environment** – being aware of sustainability issues and how you treat your surroundings

10. **Reputation** – what you stand for and your personal effectiveness

"You can't always control the wind, but you can **control** your sails."

Anthony Robbins

2.10

Celebrate success

On what can be a long and tough road to success, celebrating your key accomplishments along the way can provide both an emotional and mental break from the effort that went into winning. It can certainly be cathartic and energising to let off steam by, perhaps, throwing a party, or treating yourself and your team to some other kind of reward in recognition of your hard work.

You should also try to get more from your reward, by building in an element of sustainable long-term personal and professional growth. If you reward yourself with a short break, for example, make time for deep reflection on what you have achieved and why you succeeded. Similarly, if you have a team behind you, then it can be productive to take them away out of the work environment, so they can relax and have fun together. This encourages bonding, and you could also incorporate some kind of teambuilding exercise, while also analysing the reasons behind the latest success.

In this way, celebrating becomes part of a commitment to ongoing improvement. The insights that come from analysing the success journey can prove to be highly motivational. It can also work wonders for building self-confidence. The boost that such celebration brings can be a contributing factor to setting bigger goals that stretch you to your limits. Success is often addictive – once people have tasted it, they are left wanting more.

Viewing celebration as launch pad to the next goal is a wise move, however avoid taking it too far as you then move into the realms of over indulgence. Dwelling too much on what you have achieved should be avoided.

Memories of celebrating victory can also act as an effective antidote when you fall short of the mark. During tough times, casting your mind back to how good success felt will help to keep you motivated.

The celebration process will help to clearly define the underpinning issues that brought about success, namely:

★ The training regime that led to success
★ The pieces of the jigsaw that delivered the result
★ What went really well, and what could be improved or done differently
★ Learning for the future

"The more you **praise** and **celebrate** your life, the more there is in **life to celebrate**."

Oprah Winfrey

Beware revelling too much in your success, as it can lead to:

★ Complacency and ignoring the competition
★ An inability to move on because of the joy associated with success
★ Arrogance and a feeling of invincibility

Celebration must follow a victory, and should leave you asking:

★ What comes next?
★ How can I go even further?
★ How do I build on what has been achieved?
★ Should I look at doing things differently to stay one step ahead?

initiative, **drive** and
reputation, fulfilment,
self belief and **passion**,
control, **priorities**,
performance,
choices

Step 3

Take Control

Having clearly defined your vision and prepared yourself mentally for your mission, there's one further step to take before you blast off in search of the stars. You need to acknowledge that, ultimately, it's down to you whether you succeed or fail, and that you will be the main driving force behind your quest.

This means that the buck will stop with you, and that you need to be ready to assume full responsibility of steering yourself towards fulfilment. Sure, there are likely to be key people who will help you to get where you want to be, but it will be down to you to choose, inspire and motivate them. Although you'll undoubtedly get expert advice and guidance along the way, all the key decisions will be down to you and you'll constantly need to take the initiative and lead from the front. So it's vital that you have the determination, dedication and confidence to take charge and become a great leader.

This chapter looks at the factors you need to consider to create this winning mindset, so that you're not only ready to meet the challenges ahead, but also prepared to take full responsibility for controlling your own destiny and steering your way to success.

3.1

Learning from experience

The pursuit of success is a journey packed with exciting new experiences and possibilities. Although you're likely to enlist the help of others along the way, the ultimate force towards fulfilling your vision is you. It is you that will make it happen, and the process of actively striving to follow your passion will itself be a learning experience.

In fact, it's vital to make yourself open and receptive to this knowledge, as it will play a key role in your personal and professional development. Much of this will be discovering yourself through how you handle and react to the challenges you will face. This voyage of discovery will reveal the real you and help you define your vision more clearly.

Although you need to be the driving force behind your ambition, making things happen isn't just about intense activity. You will also need to take the time to reflect on what you've done, to assess with clarity what is and is not working. For example, when faced with adversity, did you meet the challenges head on, accept them and then re-navigate, rather than accepting defeat?

Your true strengths, weaknesses and limitations become clearly apparent when you are presented with difficult situations – such as losing your job, an unsuccessful business pitch or bad health. It is these life events that form who you are, what you believe in and what is important to you. You must frame your mindset in readiness to cope with these challenges – when adversity strikes, successful people refocus and move on with high levels of energy. Activity never ceases.

Valuable learning experiences and personal discovery comes from a constant stream of activity focused towards delivering your goal – some intense, some less so. By taking charge and making things happen, you will be in control of your destiny.

From adversity comes wisdom

Your life will be filled with ups and downs. This is a fact!
Keep telling yourself that the challenges and hurdles you
face are merely pointers on how not to do things.

Always:
★ Reflect on how you dealt with situations
★ Think about how you treated other people – both good
  and bad
★ Look for patterns in what went well and what did not
★ Don't dwell on things that never happened

"Only the paranoid **survive**."

Anthony S Grove

You should aim to keep a diary or journal of events.
By doing this you should keep a written record of your
experiences – the ones you can reflect on in quiet moments.

"A moment's **insight** is sometimes worth a life's experience."

Oliver Wendell Holmes

3.2

Building a reputation

As you strive for success, you must excel at your given vocation, talent or field of expertise. This is called functional mastery – the practice of being a recognised contributor or expert in your chosen sphere of activity. It will help you build a strong personal reputation, as well as credibility, both of which are vital components of the success jigsaw. When you exhibit high degrees of functional mastery, others will respect and value your opinions and trust your judgement.

All too often people expect others to accept their views, without displaying any substance to enhance their credibility. This makes it difficult for people to put any weight on what they say or take it seriously. A lack of credibility will inevitably lead to an uphill struggle for success.

On the other hand, building a great reputation will support personal endeavours when your peer group, team or individuals need to be turned to your way of thinking. If people respect your credentials and your expertise in your chosen field, then they are far more likely to listen to your views, take on board your comments and advice, act on it and help you on your way.

However, it takes time and effort to build a good reputation, and this is something that only you can make happen – it is certainly not built overnight. Not only do you have to learn the necessary skill, but you also have to deliver. Fulfilling on your promise is what people remember you for.

Ultimately, your reputation becomes your licence to engage with others. It will attract other likeminded individuals and help to build relationships with those that can help you on your way.

> "It takes many good deeds to build a good **reputation**, and only one bad one to lose it."
>
> *Benjamin Franklin*

Do you have a great reputation – are you a functional master?

- ★ Are you positively acknowledged and respected by your peer group?
- ★ Are you immersed in your chosen field?
- ★ Do you excel in your trade or profession?
- ★ Is it evident that you are making a difference to your team or community?

> "Reputation is only a candle, of wavering and uncertain flame, and easily blown out, but it is the **light** by which the world looks for and finds **merit**."
>
> *James Russell Lowell*

3.3

Confronting your fears

Virtually anyone that has succeeded in their profession, career or sport has had to overcome their inner fears and anxieties. These will be personal to you, and you need to take action to overcome them or run the risk of them holding you back from what you want to achieve.

In many instances, fear is an emotion you create in your own mind and it often results from a lack of confidence in your abilities to handle situations or anxiety about the outcomes. This leads to worry and negative thoughts, acting as a barrier to personal progression. The emotional turmoil created by fear stunts your personal growth, imposes limits on your beliefs and leads to a lacklustre performance that will restrict you from achieving your aims.

Getting into the habit of confronting your fears will give you the chance to prove to yourself what you are capable of and help you to release your negative thoughts. This allows you to move forward towards your vision.

You'll need to condition your mind to overcome the fears that hold you back, by getting into the habit of listening to and acknowledging them, and then questioning how real they are. Once you have taken positive steps to embrace your fears and overcome them by proving to yourself that they are only in your mind, almost anything becomes a possibility.

"Feel the fear and do it **anyway**."

Susan Jeffers

The fear factor

Fear comes in many shapes and forms. It could be:

★ Fear of failure due to the embarrassment it could result in

★ Fear of being unable to provide for your family

★ Fear of speaking in public

★ Fear of financial disaster

★ Fear of losing your job

Do away with those fears by:

★ Forcing yourself to take action against them

★ Visualise the outcome you want – not the fear factor

★ Ask yourself: how real is the fear?

★ Dispel the invisible audience that fear creates in the mind

★ How much do you want success? If you can't do away with the fear, disappointment will result

"To **conquer** fear is the beginning of **wisdom**."

Bertrand Russell

3.4

Make choices not sacrifices

When you've made the decision to dedicate yourself to striving to fulfil your vision of what you want to do in life, then you've made a choice to follow that path and deal with the challenges it presents. This will change your life from how it was before or how it would have been if you weren't following your passion. There are likely to be certain luxuries or other things that you may have to give up in pursuit of your vision.

This may lead you to feel sorry for yourself and dwell on the sacrifices you are making in trying to realise your dream. However, it's important that you quickly put this line of thinking into perspective, and realise that you feel more fulfilled than you would have done in your old life, and that you will ultimately reap the rewards of whatever hardships you may be facing by being far more successful. Essentially, what you have done is made a choice to take control of your destiny, and this should be seen as positive step and not a sacrifice.

Thinking that you're making sacrifices to pursue your goals can place a negative rather than positive slant on your mission, and can have a demoralising effect on your mind. This can translate directly into your actions, which will suffer as a result, as you're likely to feel under pressure. Constantly reminding yourself what you have given up in your quest for your vision can prove emotionally exhausting, using energy that should be focused on what you're striving for.

Ultimately, this is self-indulgent, so don't let self-pity take control of your thoughts. Success will provide you with the freedom to live your life the way you want – so focus on the prize and not the denial.

Don't wallow in self-pity

Eliminate any thoughts that you are making a sacrifice by:

★ Reminding yourself why you embarked on the journey in the first place

★ Telling yourself that it will all be **worth it** in the end

★ Being clear that you made the right decision in the first place

★ Communicating with your support network – key friends, family and colleague – who will help give you the **reassurance** that it's all worth it

★ Focusing on all the positive things you've achieved and/or plan to achieve, to put your journey into perspective against your old life

★ Thinking about how much more **control** you have over your life and how much more fulfilled you feel since you embarked on your mission

For many of us the ability to make choices is an extremely liberating emotion – you must adapt to this positive positioning of your mind. Short-term pain will lead to long term gain.

"Successful people make **choices** not sacrifices."

Anonymous

3.5

Believe in yourself

Another key factor you need in your personal armour as you battle for success is self belief. If you don't believe in your own abilities to succeed in your chosen mission, then there's little chance that anyone else will.

There is no point following your dream unless you are 100% certain you can succeed. The mindset you start off with will largely dictate whether you are going to fulfil your aspirations. So, if you keep telling yourself you can succeed, then you probably stand a good chance of doing so. The converse is also very true. If you don't have self-belief, your self-confidence will be low and you'll lack drive and purpose. The believe you can (BYC) mindset is crucial in delivering your vision.

Starting out with self-belief is vital, but events can conspire to damage this positive mindset. Channelling your thoughts into positive words and actions that are aligned with the goals you set will help you to keep on believing in yourself.

The BYC philosophy should become integral to your everyday life. If, as part of your career or profession, you manage or lead teams of people, it is your responsibility to embed such a thought process. No successful team ever wins without starting off thinking that it can!

Getting new projects and initiatives off to a flying start can really help propel you towards your goal. This requires high levels of motivation and energy to mobilise resources. When teams are involved, first ensure everyone knows where they are going and, second, that there is a collective belief that success is attainable. Teams that don't engage the BYC philosophy will be at a serious disadvantage.

However, it's important to remember that BYC starts with you! You need to foster the right climate to get the successful outcome.

BYC: Believe You Can

"It's lack of **faith** that makes people afraid of meeting challenges, and I believed in **myself**."

Muhammad Ali

Treat 'believe you can' as a personal mantra. This will boost your self-belief and drive you forward when you need that extra push. Keep repeating the mantra and:

★ It will sink into your subconscious mind
★ Provide a key source of motivation
★ Help the right activities fall into place
★ Point you in the right direction
★ Act as an antidote to negative thoughts

"You have to **believe** in yourself, that's the **secret**. Even when I was in the orphanage, when I was roaming the street trying to find enough to eat, even then I thought of myself as the **greatest** actor in the world."

Charlie Chaplin

3.6

Don't be a victim

Blaming other people when things don't go to plan or you fail is very tempting, because it's a way of absolving yourself from any responsibility. Suddenly, you're the victim, which implies there was nothing more you could do and that the failure wasn't your problem. You can make yourself feel even more helpless by being convinced that someone was actually sabotaging your hard work and efforts.

This mentality can take you to only one place – nowhere. The reality, of course, is that good things and bad things happen to everyone – that's life. But if look through the eyes of a victim, you will feel hard done by and believe that life is punishing you. This can make you bitter and angry, and you'll end up blaming everyone else for your misfortune, rather assuming responsibility yourself.

The big problem with this approach is that instead of looking for the reasons behind your failure and then setting about finding a solution, you'll simply waste your time complaining and not learn anything from the experience. Such people attract others with the same mindset, mixing a dangerous cocktail of negativity that stifles personal progression.

By accepting that you are not a victim – either of any individual or circumstance – you can begin to look for the real rea sons behind your failure. This can help you find a possible solution and will give you a better chance of success next time round. What's more, the whole experience becomes a learning process and will help you develop personally and professionally. Meanwhile, assuming responsibility will engender admiration and respect in those around you, and act as a motivational tool. Don't relinquish your control of a situation by falling victim to the victim mentality.

> "Affliction comes to us, not to make us sad but **sober**; not to make us sorry but **wise**."
>
> *H. G. Wells*

You can take some very simple steps to get rid of the victim mentality:

★ Don't feel sorry for yourself if things go wrong

★ Embrace the philosophy that life owes you nothing and success – or failure – is down to you

★ When things go wrong, ask yourself what you would do differently next time

★ When you are tempted to blame others, tell yourself that you need to assume responsibility so that you can move forward and find a solution

★ Rather than thinking: "Why does this always happen to me?", change your mindset to "What went wrong, and how can I remedy it next time?"

Show that you're big enough to assume responsibility, do away with victim mentality and see failure as a learning process that will simply mean you'll be stronger next time.

> "Feeling sorry for yourself, and your present condition, is not only a **waste** of energy but the **worst habit** you could possibly have."
>
> *Anonymous*

3.7

Ready for the challenge

No matter what you're up against, you need to give yourself the best possible chance of success. This means that you need to do plenty of preparation to make sure that you're ready for the task ahead. This will have the effect of building your self-confidence, while helping to maximise your performance.

Failing through lack of preparation can be very frustrating, because it not only delays your journey to realising your vision, but as you know you could have done better, it also throws up a number of "what if's", which can lead to regret and leave you demoralised.

What you're aiming for is the ideal performing state – the point at which your mind is perfectly aligned to the task you need to undertake. It is vital that we get our mind and body into this state before we take on any challenging situations. All your actions will flow from your state of mind, so it is important to condition your thoughts to the outcome you want. By doing this, you programme yourself to deliver a highly tuned and positive performance.

Assessing your ideal performing state takes practice, and as you move towards your goals you will need to be constantly aware of the need to be in the zone. It may be an interview for a new job or promotion, a big pitch, a marathon run or a speech you have to deliver – whatever the challenge you must connect thought and action to get the best result.

"I am the **greatest** of all time."

Muhammad Ali

Are you in the zone?

To attain the ideal performing state, you should consider some of the following mind practices:

- ★ Visualise and very clearly define what a great performance looks like for you
- ★ Work through the start, middle and ending of the task you are going to perform
- ★ Look in the mirror and tell yourself that the performance will be fantastic
- ★ Be sure to have practiced and rehearsed – winners don't wing it
- ★ Breathing can help immensely – sit upright and still, close your eyes, take a deep breath and count to seven, then slowly release and count to eleven. Repeat for a couple of minutes
- ★ Concentrate on the task at hand and avoid having your mind cluttered with other thoughts

Your ability to access the **ideal** performing state will increase your success rate. Keep practicing in the mind gym and watch yourself grow in **confidence**. Success will become habit!

"Accept the **challenges** so that you can feel the exhilaration of **victory**."

George S. Patton

3.8

Think now

Although it pays to prepare thoroughly for any task you do, taking this to extremes will only slow you down and could be confusing. The best approach is to look at the information to hand and the skills at your disposal, then plan a course of positive action. Looking too deeply into the past or worrying about the future can cloud your thinking and affect your focus.

Planning ahead is important, and you do need to consider the milestones on the route to realising your vision. But becoming preoccupied with what might happen is a waste of your valuable energy and can raise your stress level for no reason. After all, you have no control over events until they present themselves to you.

The same goes with looking back at previous encounters and analysing their outcomes too closely. At the point of failure or success, it's definitely wise to look at the factors that came into play to inform your future performance. But overly dwelling on past successes can breed arrogance and an invincibility complex, whereas harbouring regrets over past failures can be ultimately self-defeating.

Analysis at the time is key, but then it's vital to move on and stay focused on the present. After a great victory or crushing defeat, most successful football managers – and players for that matter – will say they will learn from the experience, but will them immediately focus on the next game. Similarly, although winning the leagues is their goal, their next game is their priority. Living for now hones your focus and preparation, while moving you on to your next task more swiftly and effectively.

"Living in the **moment** means letting go of the past and not waiting for the future. It means living your life **consciously**, aware that each moment you breathe is a **gift**."

Oprah Winfrey

Focusing on the present

How to think in the now:

★ When confronted with a difficult situation, look at the facts to hand and deal with it
★ Stop looking for answers and reasons – just accept!
★ Try to avoid emotional responses to a situation – think rationally
★ Don't look back if you made a wrong decision – move on
★ Be consciously aware of your thoughts and emotions

Living in the present enables you to:

★ Make quicker decisions
★ Deal with situations and circumstances more effectively
★ Achieve more in less time
★ Feel more accomplished in your work

"Children have neither a past nor a future. Thus they **enjoy** the **present** – which seldom happens to us."

Jean de la Bruyère

3.9

Doing the right things

A key part of your role in making things happen is to separate the must-do activities that are vital to realising your vision, from the nice-to-do tasks that serve a useful purpose, but are not critical to your project. As your journey progresses, and you make more contacts and, perhaps, build a team around you, there's a temptation to get involved in the nice-to-do or pet projects. The reason for this is because they tend to be less hassle and easier to fulfil in comparison to the weightier and more important must-do tasks. What's more, you may be talked into helping a colleague with a project that is important to them, but will not actually help you on your mission.

The ability to remain focused is a key ingredient for anyone who aspires to achieving more. And you'll need all your resolve to channel your focus away from the side projects that can deflect your attention from your main purpose.

Be aware of what you are undertaking. Keeping asking yourself: "Is what I am doing really going to take me where I want to be?" This level of awareness allows you to do away with non-value-added activities.

Remember, time is the most precious commodity for anyone who wants to succeed. Focusing all your attention on the must-dos rather than wasting valuable time on the nice-to-dos will help you to do the right things at the right time. Momentum results from focusing on the activities critical to success. Don't be distracted.

Must-do or nice-to-do

"The key is not to prioritise what's on your schedule, but to **schedule** your **priorities**."

Stephen Covey

Here's how to focus on the job at hand:

★ Identifying the activities vital to accomplishing your goals will help you focus

★ Keep a journal or complete a daily to do list to monitor your progress

★ Don't be distracted by other people's side projects, even though they may be important to them

★ Avoid wasting time on tasks that may be enjoyable over ones that are critical

Continuous attention on the wrong things will lead to ineffective performance and will ultimately delay your success

"I never see what has **been done**; I only see what **remains to be done**."

Marie Curie

3.10

The driving force

To achieve success through following your passion, you need to realise that this is a personal journey and that only you can make it happen. You will enlist the help of other key people along the way to help drive you forward, but you will be the primary force. As such it's vital that you take full responsibility for your actions and pursue goals with a focus and energy that is linked directly to your passion for the things you love doing.

There are three key factors that will determine your level of success, and how you are progressing towards your vision, and they rely on you personally: purpose, action and mental strength.

The **purpose** of what you are trying to achieve (and why) must be clear to you. It becomes both a driver and a motivator for your life and ambitions. Having a sense of purpose enables you to enjoy sustainable personal growth. It provides the source of energy for action planning and, more importantly, what needs to be done!

Without **action** nothing happens. All too often individuals become frustrated by a lack of progression towards their goals – the main cause of this is inactivity. Take action and then observe the feedback that results. It will reveal so much about your ideas, aspirations, strengths and weaknesses. Be sure to not only listen and observe, but also reason from the feedback received.

Mental **strength** keeps you going when you feel like giving up. Knowing what you want from your life and career is a critical ingredient of the Success Factor. Your mental toughness will be the acid test as to whether the goals you have set yourself are truly what you want. If you want success, you will keep going no matter what has been thrown in your way.

You need to stay focused on performing well in all three areas to progress as quickly as possible to realising your dream.

"Life is a **promise**; fulfill it."

Mother Theresa

The Success Factor can be viewed through the Equation for Success, where the variables are a function of what is important to you along with how you both think and operate:

Success = Purpose x Action x Strength

Anything multiplied by zero equals zero. Consequently, if you excel in each of these three areas, you will almost certainly drive yourself closer to accomplishing your mission

Take time out to **review** and think through where you are on your journey. If you are not getting the right results, put together an **action plan** on what needs to change

"Good work **habits** help to develop an internal toughness and self confident attitude that will **sustain** you through every adversity and temporary discouragement."

Paul J. Fleyer

action, **trust,**
opportunity and
credibility, capability,
recognition, **respect,**
promises,
competition

Step 4
Get Started

It's important to take time to distil your vision of success from your passion, map out the journey ahead and then make sure you're in the right frame of mind to give it everything in pursuit of your dream. However, all the careful thought and preparation in the world won't deliver the success you're looking for unless they are backed by positive action.

This means that it's crunch time. It's the moment to launch yourself along the journey you've been planning – the road to fulfilment and happiness, where you're following your passion to get you where you most want to be in life. This is the point at which you start moving forward and don't stop until you've reached your destination.

Of course, there are a lot of ways you can take action and channel your passion and purpose that will affect the speed at which you hit your goals along the way and how sustainable your success will be. This chapter looks at the key factors that will affect the effectiveness of your actions, how they may influence your journey and how you can use them to accelerate along the road to realising your vision.

4.1

The think/do balance

With the planning and preparation behind you, now's the time for action as you launch yourself on the journey of a lifetime towards your vision. Keeping up the momentum is vital to make constant progress and avoid stagnation, and it will also help you maintain your purpose and focus.

Although you need to keep moving forward, it's important that this doesn't become frenetic, but that you keep control and train your eye firmly on the prize. This means, despite the emphasis on doing, you'll also need to plan and review your actions.

The key is to allocate time to thinking and doing in the right proportions, as this will significantly increase your chance of success. To keep the emphasis on action, a maximum of 20% of your time should be dedicated to gaining clarity of thought to enable you to plan, review and strategise, while the remaining 80% should be devoted to doing. This will allow you time out to make sure you're on the right track and are learning from your experiences.

But as you're only spending a fifth of your time thinking, make the most of it. Give due consideration to the quality of your thoughts, as crisp and clear thinking will drive your plans in the right direction. Make provision for quality thinking time (QTT) – the space to ponder without interference or distraction. Thinking in stressful, chaotic conditions will achieve little.

Although focusing mentally is vital, don't be tempted to overdo it – stick to your 20% time allocation. Avoid pontificating about your desires and needs. Be sure to get on with it when you have decided exactly what it is you are going to do.

Positive progress is only made when doing follows thinking. However, your dreams and visions will remain in your head if you don't push yourself towards implementation. Remember the following equation:

Thoughts + Doing = Results

"Far and away the **best prize** that life has to offer is the **chance** to work hard at work worth doing."

Theodore Roosevelt

Quality thinking time (QTT)

A hectic lifestyle resulting from trying to balance work, family, relationships and career can make finding QTT a challenging task. The following steps will help you make space and maximise your mental performance:

★ Work out how much time you need to spend on thinking (ideally 20% of the overall time you're spending on reaching your goal)

★ Plan the time into your diary – either in one chunk or shorter periods (but make sure they're long enough, or you'll achieve nothing)

★ Find a safe haven where you won't be distracted from your thoughts

★ Make a list of key issues to consider beforehand

★ Note down your thoughts during these sessions or record them by talking into a Dictaphone to make sure your catch all your key musings

★ Use a journal to capture your thoughts and ideas

4.2

Back up words with actions

The ability to deliver what you set out to achieve and what you promise to others will have a massive impact on your reputation – it's how others will judge you. It also becomes a barometer of credibility, trust and capability. When you produce winning results, you will have a positive impact on those around you. This in turn attracts positive situations and people.

You're following your passion, so you should be enthusiastic about what you want to achieve and excited by the prospect of success. This can really rub off on others, who will be attracted by your energy and purpose. But you need to be careful what you say to people and who you say it to, as you don't want to gain a reputation for being all talk and no action. People could well hold you accountable for your comments if you don't come up with the goods, so avoid getting carried away and make sure you can back up everything you say.

Successful individuals develop a strong reputation for delivering results. Sports stars win trophies, great teachers ensure their pupils get top grades, and leading entrepreneurs build profitable businesses.

But it can be all too easy to wax lyrically about what you're going to do, without thinking of the consequences of not measuring up. Consistent failure to deliver on promises is a common feature of under performers and of individuals who lack credibility.

Always erring on the side of caution and under-promising will mean you'll frequently over-deliver. This will make you stand out from the crowd and position you as a credible individual who goes about their life with a focus on delivering results.

> "The more you are willing to take **responsibility** for your **actions** the more **credibility** you will have."

Brian Koslow

Delivering on your promises

Backing up your words with results **strengthens** your reputation and builds **credibility**, but to achieve this you need to carefully manage other people's expectations by:

★ Always being careful what you say and how you say it – don't appear boastful or arrogant

★ Considering who you're speaking to before you open your mouth – tailor your message to the individual

★ Never over promising – or you're in danger of under-delivering and letting people down

★ Always erring on the side of caution – so you will exceed expectations

★ Talking realistically about past performance – and avoiding bold future predictions

> "Under promise and over **deliver**."

Tom Peters

4.3

Review your performance

Although you may be working hard to realise your vision, if what you're doing isn't productive then you won't be getting any closer to your goal – or certainly not progressing as quickly as you could be. That's why it's important to regularly review your performance in line with your goals, otherwise your actions can become disconnected from your vision and pull you off course.

Successful people constantly evaluate their performance to assess whether they are on track to achieve their goals. They take nothing for granted and complacency never creeps into their mindset.

Complacency and a dangerous sense of invincibility can set in when you achieve a string of ongoing successes, as your mind becomes conditioned to accept winning as the norm. However, sustainable long-term success is highly dependant on remaining connected to our purpose and goals. This means you should regularly take stock of how things are going.

Constantly reviewing your performance and your environment will not only ensure you're on course, but will also help to provide you with the necessary foresight to be able to anticipate future challenges and unexpected situations – and to prepare for them.

You must develop a mechanism for sense checking both your thought processes and the activities you implement in pursuit of your ambitions. Irrespective of whether you fail or succeed, you must keep your finger on the pulse of your progress.

"The most powerful agent of **growth** and **transformation** is something much more basic than any technique: a **change of heart**."

John Wellwood

Continuous personal improvement comes from regularly reviewing progress. Take time out to think through how it's going and how you can get better. Your inbuilt review process should ask:

★ Why did I get the outcome?

★ What did I do right and wrong?

★ What external influences contributed to the outcome?

★ What things could I have controlled more effectively?

★ What are the strengths I need to build upon?

★ What can I learn from the outcome?

"If someone is going down the wrong road, he doesn't need **motivation** to speed him up, he needs **education** to turn him around."

Jim Rohn

4.4

Dealing with diversions

Ideally, you want to get to your destination as quickly as possible so you can successfully realise your vision, and that's why passion, purpose and focus are so important. However, you also need to acknowledge that the route to realising your vision is unlikely to be particularly straightforward.

You may come across barriers that you simply can't negotiate, or you may find that you get blown off course by certain circumstances. These could either be down to your own personal error or events beyond your control. If you accept that such a situation can arise, and prepare your mind for the possibility, then you'll be more likely to be able to navigate your way around the problem and get back on course. Diversions are likely to occur, so if you're open to the fact, you'll spot the problem more quickly, deal with it and get back on track, delaying your mission for as little time as possible.

Although finding that you've been diverted away from your vision can be distressing, it's important to handle any diversions from your goal in a proactive and rational way. You should avoid getting too emotional or upset about the setback and try to keep your stress levels to a minimum, so you don't add to the challenges that already exist. What's more, excess anxiety will cloud your mind and make it more difficult think straight and plan your way out of the problem.

Realise that this is only a minor setback and keep a cool head so that you can start re-planning your route sooner rather than later.

> "It is better to **light** one candle than to curse the darkness."
>
> *Chinese Proverb*

Resetting your internal compass

A good way of looking at the problem of having to deal with a diversion on your route to success is to view your **mindset** as one that operates like a satellite navigation system. No matter what happens, if you've carefully considered your vision, then your **destination** is fixed no matter what happens during your journey. When you take a wrong turning or come up against an immovable obstacle, a satnav system will simply recalculate a **new route** for you to take – and you need to take the same approach. Ideally you want to get where you want to be as quickly as possible, but taking a detour along the way will still get you there. In fact, over time you're likely to develop a compass-like mindset that automatically shifts your actions to a **new pathway** when the need arises.

> "People are always blaming their circumstances for where they are. I don't believe in circumstances. The people who get on in this world are the people who **get up** and **look** for the circumstances they want, and if they can't find them **make** them."
>
> *George Bernard Shaw*

4.5

Chase success not money

As you spring into action in the quest for your vision, it's important to dedicate 100% of your efforts to achieving your dream. If the route is not as direct as you may wish, with failures to overcome and barriers to negotiate, you are still heading towards the ultimate prize. It's also important to make sure that you keep your vision and values intact, so that when you reach your goal, you can enjoy it to the full with a clear conscience that you achieved it in the right way.

There's one factor associated with success that cannot only easily distract you from your journey, and deflect your efforts away from your vision, but also dull your sense of triumph on completion of your mission – and that's money.

Being solely motivated by money will blind you to your original vision, and you will veer off in pursuit of monetary gain to the detriment of your real dream. So bright is money's light and so strong its pull, that you can still believe you're on course to fulfil your vision, whereas in fact all your energy is being dedicated towards accumulating as much cash as possible. The problem is that, as you can never have enough money, there is no end game or ultimate fulfilment.

In your quest for money, you'll overlook the importance of relationships and the needs of others. It can fuel greed, jealousy, insincerity, selfishness and deception. Anyone solely motivated by financial gain runs the risk of alienating themselves from others and being viewed as self-centred and inconsiderate. No matter how successful you are at accumulating riches, is this real success?

Financial gain could well be a byproduct of your journey towards achieving your vision, and can certainly help fuel your quest, but you should always see it in this way and make sure your efforts are focused on realising your real dream, as that is where the real satisfaction lies.

> "Make **money** your God and it will plague you like the **devil**."
>
> *Henry Fielding*

Money can't buy your vision

Accumulation of money often plays an important part of an individual's motivation for success. Wealth often implies freedom to do what we want. If you are an ambitious entrepreneur or employee, you will want to ensure that your **rewards** are met with the appropriate remuneration package. While an important consideration, you must **balance** your focus on monetary reward with that of **success** and **achievement**. Money can be a key tool in getting you closer to achieving your vision. But this is only how it should be viewed. It should not be seen as a goal in itself.

> "The **darkest** hour in any person's life is when they sit down to plan how to get money without **earning** it."
>
> *Horace Greeley*

4.6

Make competition irrelevant

Depending on what you're striving for, on the road to success you are likely to face competition in some shape or form. The positioning that you adopt towards your rivals will invariably lead to you being compared to them. While there is a need to maintain a healthy respect for what your competitors do, you must also ensure you don't just become a 'me too' alternative – just part of the crowd. Taking the time and effort to differentiate yourself clearly from others will provide a major boost in your mission towards your goal.

Conventional wisdom teaches us to benchmark ourselves against the competition, particularly in relation to propositions, performance, approach and achievement. But if you use competitor comparisons to shape your strategy, you will run the risk of failing to capture the imagination of your target group or stakeholder community as you will be viewed as one of the pack. You must avoid being just another 'player'.

Long-term sustainable success is achieved when you align your unique qualities and offerings to that of unfulfilled needs of your audience. Paying too much attention to what your competition do will lead to you merely replicating their approach.

By developing such a mindset you start to view opportunities from the perspective of latent need rather than merely satisfying existing demand. Chasing competitors will feel like you are running the race constantly looking over your shoulder – eventually you will be tripped up.

"The ability to **learn** faster than your competitors may be the only sustainable competitive **advantage**."

Arie de Geus

Dare to be different

New thinking suggests you should almost make the competition irrelevant by:

★ Being truly **unique** in what you do and offer
★ Providing propositions that go the extra mile
★ Delivering an engaging and unexpected experience that leaves a lasting positive impression
★ Providing service that demonstrates a **genuine** desire to make a difference

Think about the needs of your target group:

★ What are the challenges they face?
★ How could you make their life easier?
★ What is currently not being provided by others?
★ What is the level of **expectation** and how can you excel?

By thinking this way you become the individual or organisation that everyone views as the thought leader, a voice of knowledge – meaning you develop a reputation for authenticity

"Taste the relish to be found in **competition** - in having put forth the best within you."

Henry J. Kaiser

4.7

Serve your apprenticeship

Harnessing your passion and sense of purpose with the aim of pursuing of your vision with real vigour will help to drive you forward as quickly as possible towards your goal. But your initial impetus will not be the one that takes you over the finish line. The key to success is learning from the multitude of experiences along the way, developing and progressing personally and professionally, and then using the new knowledge and skills to drive you further forward and accelerate the process.

To truly appreciate success, you need to be ready for it. As such, it's wise to serve your apprenticeship, as you will then be more able to cope with your achievements and press on beyond them to even greater things. Getting there too soon and not putting in sufficient effort will mean you won't reap the maximum rewards from your success.

Too many people strive for the glory long before it is deserved. Individuals that lack self-awareness often seek reward, praise and financial gain even though they have failed to reach the required levels to justify their desires. This is a common behaviour of those that don't want to put time and effort into developing themselves and their goals.

Maintain your focus on what is important and the goals you have set yourself. The limelight and the glamour can be extremely seductive. They can also override our genuine intention. Receiving the award of achieving your vision is an extremely rewarding payback from life. It also nourishes your sense of purpose. Being recognised for what you have achieved provides a spiritual boost and becomes an extremely motivating force to inspire you to want to go on and achieve even more.

"Don't worry when you are not recognised, but strive to be **worthy** of recognition."

Abraham Lincoln

Don't play leapfrog

Real **recognition** comes with having served your apprenticeship and genuinely developing a reputation as a master of what you do. People turn to you, consult and ask for your views because you are **credible**. When you try to leapfrog the learning and development process that sits before the award, you run the risk of losing credibility and not being taken seriously. Avoid being viewed as a time waster. Successful people earn the right to being awarded the trophy, but they get it in the right order – **succeed first** then seek the **applause**.

"There are two things people want more than sex and money... **recognition** and **praise**."

Mary Kay Ash

4.8

Beware short cuts

Although you'll want to get to where to you want to be as quickly as possible, it's important to dedicate all your efforts to acquiring the skills and experience you'll need to succeed, rather than spending your time thinking up quick fixes or short cuts.

"Get rich quick" and "easy" routes to success have dominated the media in recent years. But the truth is that they create unrealistic expectations for the naïve individual. If something seems far too good to be true, then it probably is. And although such a scheme may appear to potentially put you on a fast track, you will invariably get derailed along the way.

What's more, if it does work, and propel you to success quickly, you're unlikely to be prepared for it. This means that you could well lose your grip on it all too easily and let it slip through your fingers. There's also the chance that, as you have not displayed the effort and commitment that most successful people have to put it in pursuit of their dream, people will view you with scepticism, making it difficult for you to gain respect and credibility.

If, in your expediency, you've also been tempted to bend the rules, you may be branded as unprofessional and even a cheat, which could severely tarnish your reputation. All of which will increase the chances of your rapid rise being followed by a dramatic fall.

Too many people waste their natural talents and fail to put in the required effort so vital for success. Taking short cuts will lead you down blind alleys. You may get lucky but the odds are definitely stacked against you. You'd be far better advised to plan your ascent carefully, so that when you reach the summit, you'll be able to stay there for the long term.

> "There are no **shortcuts** to any place **worth** going."
>
> *Beverly Sills*

Firm foundations

Working smart to secure long-term success is what you should be trying to achieve, this means:

★ Managing your time **effectively**
★ Being clear on what strategies will avoid wasted effort
★ Constantly challenging your approach
★ Reminding yourself of the **goals** your have set
★ Being part of the community that can help you achieve what you **desire**

Condition your mind to working intelligently. This means making time for:

★ Thinking and reflection
★ Self development and learning
★ Hard work executed in a smart way

By implementing such simple, but solid, foundations, you will excel in anything you programme your mind to achieve

> "**Champions** know there are no shortcuts to the top. They **climb** the mountain **one step at a time**. They have no use for helicopters!"
>
> *Judi Adler*

4.9

Seize the moment

A vital part of taking action in pursuit of your vision is recognising when to act and having the courage of your convictions. It's one thing spotting an opportunity that could potentially accelerate you towards your goal, but it's quite another to understand that you have accumulated the necessary tools to make the most of it and then to act quickly and decisively before it disappears.

It can be too easy to let opportunities pass you by. You may be too wrapped up in planning another activity to see the signs. Fear of the risks involved may cause you to hesitate too long, so that you miss the opportunity – or even more frustrating, someone snatches it from under your nose. You may be worried about looking foolish in front of your friends, colleagues and peers should you go for it and fail.

The reality is, however, that you are likely gain respect for having a go, whether you win or not. Furthermore, the more practice you get at trying to grab opportunities when they arise, the greater your chances of success. So in many cases you will have to steel yourself, push through your comfort zone and do the things that don't come naturally in order to seize the moment.

There is a fine line between success and failure that can be as simple as taking action or not. So you must constantly remind yourself that if you want to achieve your goals it won't happen if you don't take advantage of the circumstances presented.

"80 % of success is down to showing up."

Woody Allen

Action points

A reoccurring finding from research into success shows that taking action is the single most important contributory factor. Successful people take action because they:

★ Recognise that goals only become a **reality** when implementation begins

★ Don't want to miss out on what they want to achieve in their life or career

★ Break through their comfort zones

★ Are true to their **purpose** – they want dreams to become a reality

★ Seize the moment because they live in the moment!

The next time you are presented with an opportunity, just go for it and seize the moment. When you train yourself to operate in this way, success becomes a habit and more opportunities come your way!

"Great minds have **purposes**, others have **wishes**."

Washington Irving

4.10

Never give up

A key factor on your route to success is determination. No matter how driven you are, how great a sense of purpose you carry with you, how much you want to follow your passion, or how clear your vision, yourmission will end before the finish line if you don't have the grit and determination to see it through. If you give up you will never achieve success, and all your previous hard work will go to waste. Although this seems like stating the obvious, it is a thought you need to carry with you and remind yourself of when you feel you can no longer carry on, using it to fuel your determination.

Giving up is not a phrase commonly associated with successful people. That's because their sense of purpose is so strong they will do whatever it takes to achieve the outcome they have defined for themselves. When you are presented with challenges, it can make you question whether it is worth continuing on your quest. When this happens to you, ask yourself how important achieving your goal is to you?

Ambitious people only see the achievements they want. This means their frame of mind does not drag them into negative emotions bringing activity to a grinding halt. You will regularly question your ability and hunger for victory – it's human nature to do so. However, you need to move on quickly, dig deep and find the necessary motivation to continue moving forwards. Disappointment will inevitably become a stopping off point on the road to success. However, be sure not to make this your final destination.

Keep affirming to yourself what you want and what you will achieve. The more you tell yourself that anything is possible, the more you will believe it yourself. This becomes an extremely powerful internal motivator that acts as an antidote for challenges and problems that you encounter along the way.

> "When the going gets **tough** the tough get **going**."

Billy Ocean

Digging deep

Determination is a highly prized attribute of the Success Factor – a force that kicks in when you:

★ Realise **how much** you want to achieve your goal
★ Understand how bad you will feel if you don't achieve the goal
★ Get **closer** and closer to getting what you want – the goal becomes more **real**
★ Have **clarity** about what you want from life and your career

As your determination becomes **stronger**, the less likely you are to give up.

> "A **champion** is someone who gets up even when he can't."

Jack Dempsen

talent, self awareness, caring, pride, values and wellbeing, communication, potential, skill, empowerment

Step 5
Build Your Team

Any successful person will tell you that working with others is vital to realising their goals. This means you must take a team approach to everything you do – whether that involves leading or being part of one. You must embrace a team and cooperative mindset – this team could be friends, family, colleagues or your own team – or perhaps a combination of all of these.

You must be honest with yourself and own up to your strengths and weaknesses. Then you need to establish where you need help. Having pinned down the skills you're looking for, it's vital that you find the people with the right talents, but also the appropriate personality. Get any of these elements wrong and rather than helping you towards your goal, your team could hinder your mission and at worst send you flying off course.

This chapter not only looks at building a team in the correct way, but also considers how you can get the most out of your existing team, so that you can more surely and swiftly head in the right direction towards your dream. After all, the closest thing to becoming a success on your own terms, is sharing it with the people who have climbed the mountain with you.

5.1

You can't do it alone

As someone who's very focused on the mission to realise your vision, you may be tempted to go it alone in your single-minded push for success. But don't forget that one of your primary goals should be to get there as quickly as possible, and enlisting the help of others can accelerate you along your path.

To achieve your aims, you'll also need to have supreme confidence in your ability. But it will also be important to acknowledge your weaknesses, so that you can plug the gaps with those people who have the necessary skills.

Taking on board both points means you must recognise that there's no need to do it all by yourself – and that by surrounding yourself with individuals who can offer key help and support, you can actually get further faster.

Deviating from your core strengths or taking on tasks that you are not equipped to deliver may cause you problems – either through wasted effort or simply failing because you don't possess the necessary skills to achieve a particular goal. Having a high degree of self-awareness will help you to identify the resources needed to accomplish your mission.

All too often individuals will try to fly solo, only to find that they become swamped by the volume of work needing to be done. This overwhelming sense of not being able to cope can create stressful situations that can seriously undermine your productivity and slow you down.

Finding the right people with the talents you need to achieve success shows that you possess a strong sense of realism and it makes perfect sense – it's not a sign of weakness, but rather of intelligence. So don't let your pride stand in the way of getting things done.

> "It is not the individual but the **team** that is the **instrument** of sustained and enduring success."
>
> *Anthony Jay*

People power

Your team is there to **support**, assist and guide you in achieving your goals. All successful people will tell you that without the input of those around them they would never have been able to realise their dreams. By nurturing the **talent** that sits within your team:

★ Your workload become lighter
★ More gets done
★ You can maximise your productivity by playing to your strengths
★ Work pressures seem far less intense
★ You have access to a greater pool of ideas
★ You reach your destination faster
★ Less stress!

So be open and honest about your knowledge and skills gaps, do away with personal pride and be sure to embrace the **skills** of trusted colleagues. **Delegation** of tasks to those who we know will deliver is a liberating feeling.

> "One person can be a crucial **ingredient** on a team, but one person cannot make a **team.**"
>
> *Karen Abdul, Jabbar*

5.2

Release the potential of your team

Although your route to success will be quicker if you enlist the right help from the right people, simply building your support group or team is not enough. To get the most out of your team – or in a work setting, maximise their productivity – and keep them on board, you need to communicate with them and manage them effectively to make sure they're motivated and content. Only then will you get their full commitment and be able to use their abilities to the full.

Empowering your people is likely to be one of the biggest challenges you'll face in pursuit of your vision. But taking time to get to know and understand your team and then thinking carefully about how best to recognise and reward them will pay dividends.

One of the big hurdles to overcome can be trusting your fate in their hands. As a highly focused and motivated individual you may well view others as not being as capable as you are. But the reality is that a key way of motivating people and teams to operate with maximum impact is to give them responsibility and make them accountable for their actions.

When individuals feel that they have ownership of a task, then there is a greater likelihood of it being successfully delivered. To effectively empower others, you need to dedicate time and energy to coaching them. So you must avoid neglecting the personal development and training of others as you strive to meet the busy day-to-day challenges of realising your vision.

You must create space for coaching all your people, ensuring they have the skills and motivation to perform the tasks that are needed to succeed. In this role, you must support others to achieve their personal goals, remembering these must be totally aligned to your mission.

> "There are two important factors in building a self motivated team of people – the **opportunity** to learn through increased effort and **trust** in the people to give the utmost **support**."
>
> *Tom Farmer*

Some simple steps can be followed in coaching others to perfo rm:

★ Focus and define – All coaching starts with a conversation. However, it is vital to hone in on specific areas that need to be addressed. Aim to define very clearly key skills that need to be developed

★ Explore the options – When the discussions become focused, explore the options and possibilities for what needs to be achieved. Challenge preconceived ideas. Lead by asking questions – don't give answers

★ Action planning – Get the detail on the table and work out what actions need to be implemented going forward. Agree goals and don't forget to write them down. There must be no confusion on what needs to be achieved

★ Remove hurdles – People will often see barriers and reasons not to change. Often these challenges are in the mind and don't really exist. You must try to help individuals remove these hurdles

★ Next steps – Agree what has been agreed. Pin down actions and deliverables within a certain timescale. Set a date to review the process and stick to it

5.3

Get the right people in the right roles

A highly effective group or team is built when the individuals involved are all playing to their own strengths. All too often the right person has wrong duties.

In building a team around you – whether personally or professionally – you must strive to allow people to do what they do best. You need to take time to place them in the correct position in the jigsaw of your route to success. When a piece doesn't fit and there is a mismatch in a person's skills and role, they will underperform. There's also a chance that they'll become demotivated, which will add to the problem.

Great care must be taken to ensure you don't shoehorn people into situations and roles that don't align with their capability. This will invariably lead to discontent and disconnection with the team's – and, therefore, of course, your – overall purpose. You should seek alignment between a person's passion and their ability, with the aims and objectives of the group.

The reality is that while people may be good at specific tasks, they may fall short on others. Or perhaps as the ambitions and aspirations of a group or organisation grow, those of an individual may change as their own priorities may shift. This can often result in a person either outgrowing a position or, in ambitious environments, not being able to keep up. This requires either redeployment of an individual or supporting them in gaining the necessary new skills.

To make sure you're making the right decisions with respect to the people who are crucial to your mission, you must remain connected to their emotional, personal and professional needs. By doing so, you'll become hard wired into individual and team dynamics – it will also help you to judge and decide what, if any, changes are needed.

> "Great organisations have people on the right bus all sat in the right seat. When this is achieved **anything is possible**."

Jim Collins

Close and personal

To become an **inspirational** leader, you need to keep close to both the individual and team mindset. This is done by gaining **insight** into people's:

★ Personal and professional ambitions
★ Key skills
★ Weaknesses
★ Motivations
★ Demotivations
★ Training and developing needs

You must be clear on what you want members of your team to do, and this must be delivered effectively.

> "The buck stops here!"

Harry S. Truman

5.4

A caring mentality

To get your people successfully helping you in pursuit of your vision, it's important that they care about what they are aiming for. They should be bound together by a force that is supportive of each other, with everyone working towards a common goal. Successful teams comprise a group of individuals all heading in the same direction with a united sense of purpose, with every member clearly understanding the role they have to play.

Caring is a powerful human emotion that engages others. Those teams that care are far more likely to achieve what they set out to achieve than those that don't. It is quite common for a successful team to be motivated by the fear of letting others down – those that matter to them, whether customers, fans, followers or family. Equally, this passion could be fuelled by respect of the leader and the other team members and a desire to support them as strongly as possible. This deep-rooted sense of caring almost acts as performance booster. When it is shared by a group of individuals, it becomes a force to be reckoned with.

Take time to reflect on your own team's performance. Is the spirit of caring truly woven through the fabric of the team? Sit down as a group and define very clearly what is it you care about? Build it into the team ethos and openly talk about it.

"From **caring** comes **courage**."

Lao Tzu

Pride and joy

Successful teams feel a great sense of pride abouteverything they do. This manifests into positive behaviours that become very apparent to anyone looking in from the outside. For example:

★ They will focus on the critical non-essentials – the small things that make a **difference**

★ Individuals will be **supportive** of each other in challenging times – both personally and professionally

★ They take time to talk and **communicate** to each other to avoid misunderstandings

★ They **respect** the views of their stakeholder groups and the community they are serving

★ **Promises** they make are always honoured

★ A common **voice** is shared by all

"If I do something caring for a **friend**, I have no doubt in my mind they would do it for me."

Larry King

5.5

Loud and clear

Effective communication lies at the heart of any successful group or team. You need to keep the lines of communication open at all times, so that people are not only clear about their roles, but also feel that they are being kept in 'the loop' about any developments. This helps people make a stronger emotional connection, while keeping everyone firmly on track.

A breakdown in communication and ineffective connectivity lies at the heart of many of the problems we face in our professional and personal lives. It's so easy to make assumptions that others know what is going on, when they don't. That's why it's vital to create space for both formal and informal chat, to avoid people being able to claim: "I never knew that."

Fortunately, we live in an era where there is no shortage of communication tools at our disposal. This also means that there's little excuse for not keeping people informed. Effective communication results from using multiple channels – talk, social media and mobile routes. But with increasingly digital and electronic means available, it's even more important that we engage personally face to face – discussing the challenges of the day, what went right, successes, new plans and ideas. This make people feel personally involved and gives them greater ownership. Sitting around the dinner table, having lunch or meeting up for a coffee – these traditional methods remain extremely powerful in building emotional and personal bonds.

This is how a sense of team spirit is created. By mixing impersonal and more intimate forms of communication, you will start to understand people more, their needs and drivers. It is surprising how much you can find out about people when you connect in this way. You can unearth possibilities you never imagined, which can drive you closer to your goals more quickly.

"When I get ready to **talk** to people, I spend two thirds of the time thinking what they want to **hear** and one third thinking about what I want to **say**."

Abraham Lincoln

You must remain constantly aware of the information needs of your people:

★ What do they need to know?
★ When do they need to know it by?
★ How should the information be communicated?
★ What is the consequence and impact of the team not knowing?

Delivering this key information through a mix of both the latest and more traditional, face to face forms of communication can have a massive impact on:

★ Building relationships
★ Fostering a sense of trust
★ Stimulating new ideas
★ Working out solutions to problems
★ Unlocking people's hidden talents

"The problem with **communication** ... is the illusion that it has been accomplished."

George Bernard Shaw

5.6

Spot the saboteurs

A group of high-energy and motivated people are vital ingredients to creating a strong sense of team spirit. When unleashed and aligned to a specific task or mission, the results can be unbelievable.

However, all too often you will experience team saboteurs. These individuals have an extremely negative influence on other members, as their personal intentions and aspirations do not necessarily connect with that of the team. They exhibit disruptive behaviour often intended to bring down the morale of the team and create problems that don't actually exist. They must be confronted as their method of operation can be extremely debilitating to the rest of the group.

Such individuals operate like a virus. They can infect the mindsets of others and undermine the positive values of the team. Whenever these individuals present themselves, their motives must be clearly understood and their actions questioned. Team viruses must be held to account and their activities stemmed as soon as possible. Allowing them too much oxygen can prove highly divisive and can have a serious negative impact on your mission to realise your vision.

It's important to handle this process with care in an open and honest fashion, as the people concerned may have friends within the team and you should avoid the risk of alienating these individuals. You need to understand what the problems are and why negativity is emerging from the team. Such negativity could impact on all concerned so issues need to be resolved quickly and effectively. Conflict must be avoided to ensure morale is positive. Dealt with in the right way the experience can actually bring the team closer!

> "A clear **understanding** of negative emotions dismisses them."
>
> *Vernon Howard*

Attacking the virus

Some simple steps can be taken to eliminate team viruses:

★ Try to understand the reason for negative behaviour
★ Confront with candour why they are behaving in such a way
★ Address as honestly as possible any issues that have been raised
★ Explain why the behaviour is unacceptable

The Success Factor offers no space for negative elements to take hold and divert momentum. First signs of such activity need to be addressed swiftly. Don't think the issue will go away, because it won't. The quicker you deal with it, the less time effort and energy you will spend worrying about it.

> "Keep away from those who try to belittle your **ambitions**. Small people always do that, but the really great make you **believe** that you too can become **great**."
>
> *Mark Twain*

5.7

Respect the views of others

As a driven individual with a clear set of goals and an unstinting belief in your own vision and values, it can be tempting to build a team in your image. This is unadvisable because you need a mix of skills that are more likely to be found through enlisting the help of a variety of people, and also because simply having 'yes men' on board will not provide an extra dimension to your thinking.

Successful teams are built on individuals with differing outlooks and opinions. Fusing ambitious mindsets with complementary team skills provides a bedrock for success. An eclectic mix of personalities and views also brings value to team dynamics. It stimulates innovative thinking and creative thought.

This will mean that you'll have to learn to tolerate people who may hold different views from our own. A melting pot of views and opinions can be vital in solving future problems quickly, and in questioning and reviewing processes to make sure you're on the best possible route to success.

This acceptance of others without judging them can also be an extremely liberating experience for your own mind. It can take your thinking into new areas and open your mind to new learning experiences. When we judge others we create our own internal dialogue that stops us from moving forward. That's why its important to remember that it's the results, not the person's views, that matter!

Encouraging people to express their views, no matter how disparate, creates an ideas-driven culture that uses all those involved to the full, while making people feel that their opinions are valued and that they are making a key contribution to the mission. Team dynamics and spirit are underpinned by the personality of the active individuals – diversity of thought must be encouraged. The key is to effectively manage the individuals and create a culture of openness, tolerance and inclusion.

> "He who wants a rose must **respect** the thorn."
>
> *Persian Proverb*

Progressive thinking

Opening our minds to the views of all members of the team will lead to a progressive and forward thinking mentality, because we will:

- ★ See new possibilities
- ★ Learn new ways of doing things
- ★ Release the potential of others
- ★ Solve problems more effectively
- ★ Address challenges successfully
- ★ Build an ethos of inclusion
- ★ Empower others to take ownership and responsibility

> "The ear of the **leader** must **ring** with the **voices** of the **people**."
>
> *Woodrow Wilson*

5.8

Defining a code

Sharing a common set of values is pivotal to the successful operation of a group or team. This is what helps to guide the behaviour of the individuals concerned. It is particularly important in channelling the efforts of a group of disparate individuals that share a common goal, but may display a spectrum of skills, views and opinions – key facets of a strong team.

Such a code of conduct acts as a moral compass that clearly points out the importance of carrying out tasks and dealing with others in a fair and honest way, while defining the correct approach to take in order to achieve this. A team that shares a common set of values will act in a way that is, first, supportive of each other, and second, tuned to achieving the desired goal.

Values provide a bedrock for ethical behaviour, while also creating a high level of consistency in terms of attitude and performance. They also provide a yardstick by which to assess both individuals and the team as a whole from an ethical and moral perspective. Values also lay a benchmark for how to deal with others inside and outside the group, which in a business environment directly influences internal harmony and external service levels.

It's vital that every member of your support group or team buys into the values laid out in your code of conduct and understands the need for them. They should be close to the hearts of everyone, consisting of ideas and beliefs individuals hold dear. This means the constituent values must be decided on by everyone concerned to create a real sense of ownership and desire to carry them through.

Value focused

It's vital to establish a **clear** and **consistent** set of **values** for your people early on that reflect your goals and the individuals involved. Here are three steps to help you get your code of conduct right from the outset:

Step 1 – What is unacceptable?

There are levels of behaviour you will regard as **important** to the **effective** operation of the team. It may be how you deal with each other or the community you are serving. For example, turning up late, not passing on information, poor communication, failing to return phone calls could be viewed as habits you want to eliminate. By **understanding** what you believe to be unacceptable, you are effectively defining a code of conduct.

Step 2 – Agree the team code of conduct

The team values should be **agreed** among the group. They must be **specific** and relate to the aims and ambitions of the team. By working out a code of conduct and writing it down, you then start to create a template that will govern the behaviour of the members.

Step 3 – Enforcing the code of conduct

It is everyone's responsibility to challenge those members of the team who don't adhere to the rule book. When you observe individuals not behaving in accordance with the code, they must be **challenged**. Over time and through rigorous **enforcement** you end up in a situation where teams become self managed.

"Men acquire a particular quality by **constantly** acting in a particular way."

Aristotle

5.9

Tuning in to wellbeing

In order to ensure that your people are firing on all cylinders and performing to the maximum, they need to be content with their roles and their environment, as well as being physically as close to their peak as possible. If a high level of wellbeing and contentment can be achieved, then you will be moving at optimum speed towards your vision, driven by the positive energy of your group or team.

The key to reaching and then maintaining this position of "team heaven" is to be in tune with the feelings of your people and the dynamics of the team overall, by staying connected to the group. If you can do this, any issues should become apparent almost immediately.

The problem here, however, is finding a balance between your position as leader, and someone who calls the shots, and also being approachable enough to be considered part of the team. Striking this balance successfully makes it far easier for you to tap into the wellbeing of your people.

You can also take this a step further by establishing yourself as someone who not only leads the team, but whose door is always open so that individual members can walk in and discuss their thoughts at any time. This not only helps keep you up to date with any issues that exist, but also gives you direct access to ideas that could shape the future success of your team.

The only way to create such a healthy culture is to be open and honest in your dealings with your team, which can be greatly helped by instilling a firm set of values from the outset that everyone can buy into.

Keeping your finger on the pulse

To help keep up with the wellbeing of your team, you need to be hooked into five critical areas:

What does 'now' look like?

The morale of the team is an important indicator of its performance. Is there a sense of being up for it? This means lots of positive energy and language that describes the state of affairs. Conversely have heads gone down? Are people clock watching and just waiting for the day to finish.

Feel parting of it

Are people connected to the purpose of the team. Is there a 'them' and 'us' attitude? Are people proud of being part of the team brand? You must aim to foster a sense of pride within the team.

Performance culture

A performance mindset drives the Success Factor. Is the team on target to deliver and are the measures showing a positive move towards achieving the goals? Are people falling short of their targets – if so what are the underlying issues?

Future connected

Is the team clear on the bigger picture in terms of longer terms aims and aspirations? To achieve sustainable success all individuals need to understand where the team is heading. This sense of belonging provides a feeling of security for individuals and it also fosters a sense of commitment.

Being Informed

Is the team informed, do they know what is going on? Are you providing feedback and highlighting issues that the team need to be aware of? If there is an underlying sense of not knowing, people will start to wonder what is going on.

5.10

Marking victories

When you and your people have achieved success, celebration must follow rapidly in recognition of your triumph. This becomes the reward for all the hard work, commitment and dedication that your group or team has put in. It serves as motivation going forward and gives the space and time to reinforce the how the success was achieved and revel in its glory.

Celebration can span the spectrum from a group cheer through to a party for all the contributors. The celebration is more than a release of emotional energy, it provides an opportunity to review everyone's performance at an enhanced level of awareness.

Given that you and your people have achieved what you set out to deliver, your relaxed state of being allows you to analyse what went well in a more detached way. While conventional wisdom tells you to learn from your mistakes, equally you must also learn from what you did well.

Part of the celebration should involve a period of reflection to distill "success insights" – those positive aspects of the performance that can be reproduced over and over again. This becomes an extremely effective way to build a stronger team bond, expertise and confidence.

It's a good idea to take time to note down the core ingredients of the success, and then circulate it to all members of your team to remind them of the key facets of achievement.

"Before the **reward** there must be **labour**. You plant before you harvest. You sow in tears before you reap in joy."

Ralph Ransom

Move on quickly

A word of caution – don't dwell on success for too long, as it can be distracting and lead to **complacency**. This in turn will create a disconnection with the reality of your day-to-day demands, ultimately delivering a less than acceptable performance. However, **celebration** can be an extremely powerful **motivator**, particularly when your people know that fun or some other form of self-reward follows achievement. However, it's vital that individuals remain **grounded** and recognise that celebration always follows **attainment**. This means that any partying must be deserved. With no winning performance, celebration is pointless and lacks purpose.

"I hate **complacency**. I play every gig as if it could be my last, then I enjoy it more than ever."

Nigel Kennedy

belief, loyalty, **connectivity, understanding, inspirational** leader, confidence, **sincerity,** feedback, **humility**

Step 6

Learn to lead

It's one thing having your team firing on all cylinders, but what if you could push your people to new heights of excellence? Then you really would be flying towards realising your vision. An athlete relies not only on themselves to set a new personal best record, but also on their coach and the training methods they use. Truly inspirational coaches create world-beating athletes. By becoming a visionary leader, you can do the same for the people around you.

However, your influence as a great leader won't simply be restricted to the boundaries of your internal network. Your reputation and kudos will act just like a magnet, drawing people to you who will help to spur you on in your mission. These could be key partners, stakeholders or customers.

In this chapter, you'll find out what it takes to become an inspirational leader, and what you stand to gain from it. Clearly, this isn't something that will happen to you overnight, unless you have particularly intuitive leadership qualities. However, it's certainly something you should aim for as you travel along your journey to success, as once you have reached the top, it can play a key role in keeping you there.

6.1

Leading yourself

If part of our journey to success involves leading others, you should first reflect on how good you are at leading yourself. Do you have a framework within which you manage and lead your life? Do you have a written statement of what you believe in or of how you want to be perceived by others?

It's important for you to have a clear set of beliefs and values, and to be disciplined enough to apply them to everything you do. This personal creed will not only help you to follow your dream consistently and effectively, but it will also dictate how you behave towards and engage with colleagues, friends and your community – the vital support system to assist you in your mission. It will provide the basis upon which you lead people, so the more ethical and honest your set of beliefs are the better. This will engender trust and loyalty – two key factors in helping your people perform to the maximum, and become a great leader.

You're more likely to achieve your quest for long-lasting sustainable success and personal growth if you have a moral compass embedded within your mindset, which governs how you lead your life and how you lead others. Although linked to your vision, your personal creed is more about what you believe rather than what you want to become. It is a statement of belief about who you are, and will therefore significantly influence what others think of you. View it as a blueprint for how to live your life and how you treat others. Carefully consider it, distill it and practice it.

Your moral compass

In constructing your own personal creed, think about the following:

★ How do you want to be of service to friends, family, colleagues and your profession?

★ What is your promise to others?

★ How do you want others to describe what you do and what you are about?

★ What are the rules that govern how you deal with others?

In developing a set of beliefs you must be precise and capture the essence of who you are. Take time out to discover the real you. This provides the right foundation upon which to lead others.

"Control is not leadership; management is not leadership; **leadership** is leadership. If you seek to lead, invest at least 50% of your time in leading yourself – your own **purpose, ethics, principles, motivation, conduct**. Invest at least 20% leading those with authority over you and 15% leading your peers."

Dee Hock

6.2

Laying the foundations

Key to attracting the right talent, motivating it to perform as best it can, and retaining it, is being an inspirational leader. To achieve this, you need the right foundations on which to base your leadership platform and ethos.

It's all about creating the best possible environment in which to lead your team and help it flourish. First, you have to make sure that the working atmosphere is conducive to getting the most from your people. How you conduct yourself will have a direct impact on your team. If you are upbeat, positive, dynamic and supportive, this will galvanise your team into behaving in the same way and drive your mission forward. People will thrive in such an atmosphere, and look forward to each day. Furthermore, as you'll be practising what you preach, you'll gain respect and encourage loyalty.

It's also vital to show you care by giving regular positive feedback, helping people develop and improve, and asking for their ideas and opinions on everything from their working conditions to strategy. To establish an open and honest culture, it's also important to make sure everyone knows what's going on, so that no one feels left out from decisions or is unsure of their role, while being fully aware of how things are progressing.

Finally, the key is consistency in all of the above, which can be achieved by laying down a strong vision for your team, along with a set of values that everyone agrees with and can commit to. This should be backed by clear, realistic targets and an agreed reward and recognition programme, along with regular performance reviews. This combination of positivity, support, encouragement, awareness and direction should help you to lead in the right way and establish a winning team.

"Leadership is intentional **influence**."

Michael McKinney

The 4Cs of great leadership

Using this framework will provide the basis of a great leadership platform:

Conditions – You must build an **environment** that others want to be involved with. It must excite and engage to maximise motivation. Always remain upbeat, celebrate successes and most of all remember the old adage: "Walk the walk and talk the talk".

Coach – Encourage others to reach their full **potential**. Show you care by understanding your people's strengths and weaknesses, and offering constructive feedback. Have a regular performance review system in place.

Communicate – Ensure that lines of **communication** are constantly open and all concerned understand what's going on. Say it how it is it and do not avoid delivering the true facts.

Conformity – Have **clear** vision and values, around which **consistent** realistic targets can be set and monitored. Playing by the rules is essential.

"The **task** of the **leader** is to get his people from where they are to where they have not been."

Henry Kissinger

6.3

Shun arrogance

Although you may start off well, with a great base for good leadership on which to build, it's important to make sure that you continue and develop this path, rather than succumbing to arrogance by letting success go to your head. It is common to see people who enjoy sustained periods of success change their attitude and find themselves repelling the people that once held them in high esteem.

Individuals that become intoxicated by their own self importance run the risk of alienating others. And when this stretches to your close group or team, it can significantly hinder future success. Such arrogance can also result in copycat behaviour in your people, creating a bad atmosphere, infecting any external dealings and putting off others.

Individuals who embrace such an arrogant approach enter a danger zone in their career and life. Peer groups will start to talk, and the word will quickly spread. Personal and supportive networks built over time can start to dismantle as people start to distance themselves.

Avoid this by remaining grounded in your life and career. Celebrate the successes you achieve, but be careful not to develop a superior positioning to others. Remember that there is a fine dividing line between confidence and arrogance. So listen to how you speak to others, how you relate to them, what you say about yourself and how you describe your achievements. Be aware of your language and how you interact with others. Empathy builds relationships and gains the respect from your peer group. Arrogance hinders personal development and friendships. So don't stray into the dark side, as people will turn their back on you.

" **Humility** is a sign of a **great** leader."

Jim Collins

Hidden dangers

It's easy to think yourself as **superior** to others once you have enjoyed a number of successes, but this is a big **mistake** as it will drive people away and severely disrupt the pursuit of your **dream**. Make sure you don't fall into the trap of displaying arrogant behaviour, the key unpleasant facets of which include:

★ Thinking you have all the answers
★ Ignoring the views of others
★ Not listening to colleagues
★ Ridiculing others who don't agree with you
★ Not taking into account the feelings of others

"**Sense** shines with a double lustre when it is set in humility. An **able** and **yet humble** man is a jewel worth a kingdom."

William Penn

6.4

Tap into key mindsets

To become a great leader and motivator, you need to build on creating the optimum environment for your people to operate in by also becoming highly connected to it and your team.

Leading a team means that connectivity is required at many different levels. As well as being in tune with the needs, views and aspirations of the people who are offering you key support in pursuit of your goal, it's also necessary to develop close links to other groups that are vital to your success. These include your audience – the customers or other groups of people that are directly buying, using or benefiting from what you are doing. Understanding their mindset means you can deliver a far better service.

Then there are those who are not part of your organisation or group, but also have an influence over your level of success. You must recognise and carefully manage the needs of these stakeholders to make the journey to realising your vision as smooth as possible.

Good, strong leadership involves acknowledging, understanding and managing all the different groups that play a part in your success. You need to develop an empathy for them and an appreciation of their thinking by listening and interpreting what you hear. Immersing yourself in these networks will provide first-hand experience of their drivers and motivators, and you'll be better equipped at delivering what they need in support of your mission.

The three levels of engagement

You must think of your environment or community of interest on three levels and follow their needs:

Staff – You need to **relate** to the people whose trust and respect you must win over. Embed yourself within your team and seek to **understand** their needs and aspirations. Showing people that you care about them goes a long way, but you must do this with sincerity.

Stakeholders – This group could be shareholders for the chief executive of a public company, or a board of governors for a headmaster. Such groups can be highly **influential** in supporting your future as they can become long-term personal connectors, satisfying and understanding their needs is vital!

Primary audience – This group represents your **target** group. For companies, it's customers, for academics it's students, and for politicians it's the voter. An ability to dig deep into the needs of your primary audience will help you to understand **current** and **future** needs.

"There are two ways of **spreading light**: to be the candle or the mirror that **reflects** it."

Edith Wharton

6.5

Leading for the long term

Creating an environment that encourages sustainable success, rather than simply looking to the short term, will not only help you move on from initially realising your vision, but will also provide the stability on which you and your organisation can thrive.

As a leader, showing that you have your mind focused as much on the long-term as you have on the present will give your people the confidence that their future is in safe hands. Consequently, they are likely to pledge their futures to you, with the dedication, commitment and loyalty that it brings.

Equally, any stakeholders will be reassured by this approach and will be more willing to commit their support or sign longer-term contracts. All of which will make a major contribution to your success.

This means that your mindset should be orientated around a "built to last" philosophy. While achieving short term goals is vital to victory, they must link into a higher purpose for life, career, relationships and family.

Real success is not transient, but is based on deep-rooted principles that want to give something back. Many organisations and individuals want to leave a legacy that will add value long into the future. To achieve this, avoid short-term gain as this can lead to long-term loss, but rather connect your thinking to the principle of sustainability.

Embrace this mentality and you will become a star of the future, savouring ongoing success and fulfilment. A long-term perspective translates into a positive human quality that attracts, engages and energises others.

"Short term **gain** – long term **loss.**"

Anonymous

The sustainable mindset

All too often, a sudden rise in success is wiped out due to:

- ★ Loss of purpose
- ★ An **inability** to accept success
- ★ Greed and wanting more
- ★ Arrogance and **disconnection from** reality
- ★ Over indulgence
- ★ **Lack** of self control

You will achieve ongoing success and growth when you:

- ★ Remain **connected** to your purpose
- ★ Are **passionate** about what you are doing
- ★ **Care** about others and remain connected with their mindset
- ★ Feel as though you are making a **difference** in what you do
- ★ Have a **vision** of what you want to achieve that remains clear in your mind

6.6

Handling tough calls

Achieving success invariably means there will be times when you will have to make some big decisions – and they're never easy. As a leader, it's vital that you are prepared for these tough calls, and carefully consider their outcome, as they can have a dramatic impact on the life of others, and your chances of achieving your goals.

You may have to make a person redundant or reprimand an individual for poor performance. In such cases, the temptation could be to avoid making those tough choices, therefore cutting the risk of being disliked by colleagues, team members and your peer group. Unfortunately, these are decisions that have to be made in order for you to realise your vision, and in some cases avoiding them can actually derail your ambitions. This means that if you have a group of people behind you, supporting your aim, they will also be disadvantaged by you not facing up to your responsibilities. There's the chance that shying away from a big decision could leave you looking weak, which can undermine your authority as a leader.

The key is to always confront challenging situations and deal with them in a professional way so that you gain respect from those around you. This involves being open and honest about the decisions you have to make, making sure that everyone's clear about the reasons behind your choice. If this involves one or more individuals, then it's vital to treat them – and be seen to be treating them – fairly and to follow the correct protocol. By doing this, you will at least gain respect – even perhaps from those who may not agree with your decision – and you'll be seen as a strong leader who is courageous enough to face up to their responsibilities for the sake of their team.

> "Successful leaders have the **courage** to take **action** while others hesitate."
>
> *John C. Maxwell*

Doing the right thing

When confronted with having to make and deliver a difficult decision, remember to:

- ★ Explain why it has been made
- ★ Deliver it with **respect** for others
- ★ Provide a commentary on how things will **change**

When decisions are based purely on the premise of being liked and not for the right reasons, you will almost certainly create further problems. Successful people gain respect from others by doing things for the **right reason**.

> "Please all, and you will please none."
>
> *Aesop*

6.7

Support and development

Effective leadership and management are woven into the fabric of achieving our own personal success. You must dedicate time, effort and resources to coaching and encouraging those individuals pivotal to you realising your ambitions. Everyone is different, and you must learn what the motivation on and off buttons are for each person. You must also adapt your leadership style to reflect the personalities of your people and the tasks they have agreed to perform.

You'll also gain a lot from the process, as supporting the personal growth and development of others is an extremely rewarding task. To feel that you have supported and made a difference to the lives of your friends, family and colleagues is an important part of your journey.

Embedding a performance culture and mindset is equally important to your daily work and life. This involves instigating simple and clear mechanisms and measurements to monitor the progress of yourself and your team. Such yardsticks must be communicated to all concerned to avoid misunderstandings.

Effectively managing others that are part of your success jigsaw means you have to address performance in different ways. For some individuals, you have to provide more of a supportive role to allow them to develop and grow. This could be a consequence of their need to acquire the skills and competencies pivotal to performing their duties.

At the other end of the scale, poor progression resulting from negative behaviours, such as laziness or lack of caring, should be dealt with in a more disciplined way. Success and attainment need to be rewarded with the appropriate praise and rewards. A mindset with such clarity gets everyone moving in the same direction. It helps you to lead others so that they support you to succeed.

"Make sure that team members know they are working **with** you, not **for** you."

John Wooden

The performance culture

Fundamental to getting people on side is developing your ability to:

★ Provide leadership by asking questions – not by providing answers
★ Enter into debate and dialogue (coercion is strictly forbidden!)
★ Review performance, but avoid blame

Individuals under your leadership must:

★ Be clear about what is expected of them
★ Understand time scales involved and key milestones
★ Appreciate the impact and consequences of not delivering

"You can **motivate** by **fear**, and you can motivate by **reward**. But both those methods are only temporary. The only **lasting** thing is **self motivation**."

Homer Rice

6.8

Making decisions

Your personal and professional aspirations should be pursued against a background of careful decision-making. In your quest for success you will be continuously faced with options – the decisions you make will directly determine the effectiveness of the direction and strategy you implement. You should always aim to make decisions on the basis of "doing the right thing" and "for the right reason" – this inspires and motivates others to follow. Such a mindset and approach will, without exception, build a loyal and dedicated following. Leadership of this nature drives 'followership'. With the right people behind you and supporting you, your journey becomes much easier.

Effective leadership means making lots of decisions, many of which will have to be explained because they impact on people's lives and wellbeing. Decision making must be based on what is best for the mission in hand – the Success Factor refers to this as "best intention" – decisions that are decent, honourable, communicated with respect and in the best interests of all concerned. Beware, not everyone will agree with your course of action.

If you are constantly analysing what impact you will have on each and every person in your community then procrastination will prevail. Under these circumstances, decision making becomes long and drawn out, nothing gets done. You then become frustrated by lack of progress towards your goals.

As long as each decision you make is guided by your own personal creed, then you can be safe in the knowledge that you have made it in the right spirit and with no intent to negatively effect others unnecessarily. However some decisions will be unpopular ones and this cannot be avoided. Trying to please everyone and explain your reasoning in detail is simply not feasible – it takes too much time and effort. It also dilutes your effectiveness as a leader.

"It doesn't matter which side of the fence you get off on sometimes. What matters most is getting off. You cannot make **progress** without making **decisions**."

Jim Rohn

The principal of best intention

On your journey towards your vision, you must lead people by following the underlying principles of best intention. These are:

★ No malice or hurt caused for others
★ Genuine desire to bring and add value
★ Avoidance of inflicting humiliation on anyone in your community
★ Free from greed
★ All decisions are made in the interests of success for all

When your mindset is aligned to that of **best intention**, you have fulfilled your moral duties to others.

"We know what happens to people who **stay in the middle** of the road. They get run over."

Aneurin Bevan

6.9

Reinforcing key messages

It's important to consistently reinforce important messages to both yourself and those you are leading to make sure key tasks are carried out on time and in the right way. This helps to keep you on track to achieve your vision. You and your people are likely to be working in a busy environment, where it can be easy to forget key information, so having a regime in place that regularly reinforces important details to help and support your team is a sign of good leadership.

When other people become part of your equation for success, it's vital to maintain regular communication that enables everyone concerned to be clear about what needs to be achieved. This can mean repeating yourself, but persistence in communicating vital messages will ultimately ensure there is united thinking – and people will thank you for keeping them on course.

When reinforcing key information, you need to make sure that you're being consistent. If not, then you may be misunderstood or cause confusion. In other words, you will be sending out mixed messages, and this could erode your credibility as a leader. Furthermore, you'll become frustrated as others start to ignore your voice.

The backbone of effective communication is a continuous feed of information delivered with clarity and consistency. When you incorporate this into your daily routine, not only will you engage with others more effectively, but you'll also find it easier to say what you want to.

Clarity and consistency

Be clear on what it is you want to communicate to others, by taking time to think through:

★ **What** you want to say
★ Why it's **important**
★ **How** you're going to say it

If it helps write it down – but make sure it is delivered in the right **tone** and in a way that ensures there is no misunderstanding. Don't run the risk of being viewed as someone who just goes "off on one" all the time.

"The **less** people know, the **more** they **yell**."

Seth Godin

"The **void** created by the failure to communicate is soon filled with **poison**, drivel and misrepresentation."

C. Northcote Parkinson

6.10

Leading by example

The quicker you can get the people around you to accept, adapt and implement change effectively, the further you'll be along your journey to success and the quicker you'll reach your destination. The best way to do this is to lead by example.

Old-school leadership promotes the practice of "do as I say, not as I do". Such a dictatorial approach runs the risk of creating resentment and disillusionment in the ranks. A more progressive approach to leadership follows the wisdom of "I won't ask you to do something that I have not done myself before or that I am not willing to do now". Such a philosophy provides the foundation for positive progression of change.

Successful people don't just use rhetoric – or talk the talk – they also back up their words with actions – or walk the walk. By implementing such a mindset, people instantly know that what you say, you will do. Taking such a stance builds your credibility, enhances your reputation, wins hearts and minds, and fosters a climate of trust and loyalty.

The world is full with people who make empty promises, so make sure that you don't fall into the trap of being superficial. Stand out from the crowd by pursing a philosophy where affirmative action follows your words. By doing so, you will inspire others to follow in your footsteps, act on your instructions and advice, and support you on your own personal mission.

> "A leader is one who **knows** the way, **goes** the way, and **shows** the way."
>
> *John C. Maxwell*

5 steps to leadership credibility

Follow these simple ways to make sure you talk the talk and walk the walk:

1. Become the **change** you wish to see. It is extremely powerful for others to observe the leaders carrying out actions and behaviours they are requesting from others.
2. If you make a rule or design a process, **follow** it, until you decide to change it. Why would others follow the rules if you don't?
3. Act as if you are **part of the team** and do what you expect from others. People will appreciate that you are personally knowledgeable about the effort needed to get the work done. They will trust your leadership because you have undergone their experience.
4. Help people **achieve** the goals that are important to them, as well as the goals that are important to you. Make sure there is something for each of you that will result from the effort and work.
5. Don't make **promises** that you can't keep. People want to trust you and your leadership.

> "**Example** is not the main thing in influencing others, it is the **only** thing."
>
> *Albert Schweitzer*

goodwill, satisfaction, honesty, integrity and admiration, openness, self control, patience, giving, first impressions

Step 7
Earn Respect

No matter how knowledgeable or skilled you are, you will find it difficult to get where you want to be if you're not liked. Although you may still be an effective leader, you're unlikely to become a great one. You may be successful to a certain extent, but you will not have the admiration and kudos to be able to sample the sweet taste of real success.

Without the goodwill of others, you will find that you have to overcome frequent barriers, making your journey a particular struggle. The key to getting people behind you is to win over hearts and minds by working tirelessly to earn respect.

On the road to success, you'll be tempted into activities that may appear to get you closer to your dream, but in reality are simply short-term tricks that will damage your reputation, lose you respect and ultimately make your mission harder. Although it can be more of an effort to do the right thing, it is likely to pay real dividends in the long term.

In this chapter, we consider the factors that can have a direct influence on your reputation and the level of respect you can garner. Doing everything you can to win the respect of others will mean you'll realise your vision more quickly, while enjoying the journey and the success far more.

7.1

Rise above envy

There is nothing quite like the feeling of achieving something. The sense of euphoria and satisfaction makes all your hard work worth it. Often, one of the first things you want to do following a success is to tell people about it, as it's great to share these key moments. But how would you feel if someone wanted to celebrate their success with you? Would you be delighted at their achievement or would you harbour resentment and jealously?

Sadly, the latter emotion is an all too common response to success. In fact, personal achievement can stimulate a whole raft of negative feelings from others. Rather than offering praise and genuine applause to those whose hard work has delivered results, all too often so called friends, colleagues and family become envious.

This way of thinking is frequently associated with the wealth and material goods that we perceive others have acquired or the accomplishments and rewards our peers enjoy. If your mindset is dominated by this way of thinking, then it is time for change. You must do away with resentment as it will consume your thoughts and distract your own efforts. It creates mental and emotional hurdles that stand in the way of you getting on with what you need to do.

If you're confident in your own ability and content in your mission to achieve your vision, then other's success should not be seen as a threat, but as something to celebrate. You should also use the victory as a stimulus for you to learn and acquire new knowledge – it provides hidden clues that can guide your own mission. Ask yourself why have they succeeded and what you can learn from them.

Genuinely revelling in the success of others will earn you respect as people will see you as magnanimous, generous and caring. It's also vital to celebrate and reward success in your support group and team, not only as motivation, but also to set the right example and gain respect and loyalty.

> "The more I help **others** to succeed, the **more I succeed.**"
>
> *Ray Kroc*

Free your mind

At a deeper level, **celebrating** the success of colleagues frees your mind from the turmoil of negativity that envy can invoke. **Acknowledging** the achievements of others is massively **motivating** for them as individuals. Just think how good you felt the last time someone said: "Well done" to you for your hard-earned triumphs. Get into the **habit** of **genuinely** congratulating those that achieve – it creates a positive energy for all concerned

What you gain from revelling in others' victories:

★ Admiration
★ Inspiration
★ Respect
★ Motivation
★ Self-pride
★ Gratitude
★ Loyalty

> "In helping **others**, we shall help **ourselves**, for whatever good we give out **completes** the **circle** and comes back to us."
>
> *Flora Edwards*

7.2

First impressions

Why do you instinctively respect some people, but others can be very hard to appreciate? Clearly, to respect someone properly, you need to get to know them well enough to gain an appreciation of what they have achieved and how they have achieved it, along with their attitude towards their friends, family and colleagues. You will also need an understanding of their values and beliefs. Yet it is still possible to feel an instant respect for someone you have only met once.

This is all down to how you deal with people on meeting them, and the first impressions you give. Projecting the right image in this way can make a major contribution to realising your vision, because first impressions stick in people's minds and are likely to make them more receptive to you during future meetings or conversations. As a result, it can help to speed through key agreements and cut down the time spent negotiating, as people are more likely to trust your judgement. It can also get your team firing on all cylinders from the start, because instantly they feel a sense of trust and loyalty towards you.

Creating the right impression early on is all about striking the right balance between quiet self-confidence, politeness, attentiveness, modesty and warmth. Openess, honesty and a self-effacing nature can also help. These are all attributes you need to embrace in your mindset to make sure your relationships get off to flying start.

Getting personal

Adhering to some simple principles will ensure that you engender **respect** in others from the first meeting:

★ **Be polite** – Treat everyone you meet in the same way. A **smile** and **polite** debate helps to break the ice with the new people you encounter.

★ **Listen** – Be sure that you **listen** to the views of others. Even when you disagree with their points, always reply in a way that is **respectful** to them and their opinions

★ **Deliver** – Ensure that you **do** what you say you will do and at all costs avoid letting people down. If you can't keep a **promise**, let others know.

★ **Be modest** – Don't **boast** about your achievements. While we can be proud of what we have accomplished, leave it to others to distribute the **praise**.

★ **Be self-deprecating** – Be **open** about your limitations and don't take life or yourself too seriously. It's a fine human quality to be able to **laugh** at yourself.

★ **Respect yourself** – recognise your **worth** and be aware of the impact you make personally and professionally. However, be clear of the fine dividing line between boasting and **modesty**.

It is important to recognise that we **earn** respect, under no circumstances should we **demand** it or take it as a given.

"A thousand words will not leave so **deep** an impression as one deed."

Henrik Ibsen

7.3

Delivering integrity

Living your life within a framework of honesty and trust is key to gaining respect through integrity, and is vital in forging important relationships that can help you get you to where to want to be. Projecting integrity will have a powerful effect on boosting your reputation, which you need to nurture and protect to achieve success. Damaging your reputation can seriously dent your ambitions. Practising honesty and trust will help you to build a sustainable and highly rewarding life and profession. Your integrity will result in others naturally gravitating towards you.

If someone gains a reputation for being "modest with the truth", then their standing within their community will suffer, as they will be seen as unprofessional and untrustworthy. The fact is that negative messages spread very fast, and once you have gained a bad reputation, it can be very difficult indeed to shake off. These days, globalisation and the increasing use of social media channels means that unsavoury behaviours can be communicated to literally thousands of people within a matter of seconds.

Success invariably means that you must build mutually beneficial relationships. These will flourish through the conditions of openness built on a commitment to trust and honesty. This helps to form the basis of highly effective partnerships and teams – ones that are motivated to succeed. You can't enter into any form of joint venture by simply asking someone to trust you. Trust must be earned, which means that a proactive commitment to honouring the pledges you make will strengthen the bonds with people who are important to you.

Avoid the time slip

Trust can take years to build, yet a single dishonest act can destroy it in seconds. Equally trust can be eroded over time, as we make small promises and never follow them through to completion. In such instances others will gradually lose faith in what we say. This slow, but constant chipping away of trust eventually leads to irrevocable damage to valued relationships. This is why it's vital for you to embed honesty, openness and ethics into your mindset, as these are the key attributes that generate trust and integrity

"What is left when honour is lost?"

Publilius Syru

Personal integrity is born out of living your life in an honest and truthful way. When combined with a purpose, it becomes a powerful driving force for success.

"If you tell the truth you don't have to remember anything."

Mark Twain

7.4

Greed is not good

The financial crises that many of the world's economies have experienced in recent years have been largely fuelled by a culture of greed and selfish behaviour. In fact, there can be no better example of the pitfalls of basing success on such unreliable foundations. They have dealt a massive blow to nations and communities across the globe, as well as ruining the lives of many in the process.

Personal philosophies, missions and strategies based on a "win at all costs" mentality have a tendency to deliver outcomes that lead to misery and suffering – and not just for the perpetrators, as the global recession has shown. Defenceless and trusting people lost everything, and through no fault of their own have had to rebuild their lives from scratch. People motivated to acquire and possess more than they need or deserve are the root cause of this saddening state of events.

Such a self-centred approach may deliver riches, but often the people who achieve success in this way will have alienated themselves in the process, making their victories rather hollow and lonely. The lack of respect that such an approach results in also makes it more difficult to recover from any setbacks along the way, as people are likely to desert you once the going gets tough. This is because they don't trust you and are not prepared to show you any loyalty.

Display greed and immediately others become wary of you and your approach to life. They become suspicious about your motives and will question your integrity. Building relationships with individuals motivated by greed can be challenging, as self-interest governs their work ethic. The true route to success and satisfaction is to create a mindset and culture that encourages a positive outcome for all and mutual support along the way.

All about you

Greed is not a particularly engaging human quality. It promotes an approach underpinned by a **win/lose scenario**. In other words, greedy behaviour more often than not leads to:

★ Another person or party losing out
★ Bad feelings
★ A sense of being cheated
★ Conflict and unrest

"It is preoccupation with **possessions**, more than anything else, that **prevents** us from living **freely** and **nobly**."

Thoreau

Avoid greed by being aware of your attitude to material goods. Don't let your mindset be **ruled** by accumulating wealth at the misfortune of others. Maintain **balance** across your material needs, otherwise you run the **risk** of losing the respect of others because you are perceived as being greedy. This will become a barrier to your advancement. Always think win – win!

"The **tighter** you squeeze, the **less** you have."

Thomas Merton

7.5

Try to be humble

Humility is a highly engaging and endearing human quality. If you're humble, you are able to connect effectively with other people, something that can play a key role in enlisting the help of others on your journey to success. This results from the personal chemistry you are able to develop quickly with other individuals.

Someone who exhibits humility is truly comfortable in their own skin – they are confident in themselves, are fully aware of their strengths and weaknesses, and treat everyone as an equal. Embedding humility in your character and mindset will provide you with a vital tool for winning the respect of others. Also by embracing this trait, you are flying in the face of the characteristics most associated with ambitious, driven individuals, such as aggression, arrogance, boastfulness and vanity. This will automatically give many people a pleasant surprise, as they find your approach a refreshing change from the norm.

To some, humility can be viewed as a sign of weakness and it is not often associated with success. However, it is a powerful and invisible force. When combined with a strong sense of ambition and professional will, it can deliver extraordinary personal progression. Furthermore, without humility, success – whether it's wealth, power or status – breeds bad feeling, fear and anxiety. Victory within the framework of humility brings harmony to individuals, teams and organisations.

In a modern world where rhetoric and egos seem to have dominated society, returning to fundamental principles of just being a nice person can only be a good thing. By incorporating this way of thinking, you will broaden your appeal to others in your community.

Broaden your appeal

When you embrace a mindset that is grounded in a sense of humility, it provides:

★ A greater self-awareness, because your ego does away with opinionated views

★ An ability to empathise with your community, as it removes any ideas of inferiority or superiority

★ A vehicle to enable you to communicate more powerfully, because your words reflect your passion and the real you

★ Opportunity for personal growth, because of a heightened state of awareness of your shortcomings

Cultivating the behaviour of humility needs to become an integral part of your success journey:

★ Study the speeches of great leaders and observe how humility is woven through the fabric of their approach to both life and mission

★ Embrace a serving mentality. By considering ourselves as serving others we groom our mind to recognise that we are doing good and adding value to those we consider important

★ Be aware of the words you use to describe your achievements. Do away with indulgent terms that appear boastful or arrogant

"We descend by **exaltation** and we ascend by **humility**."

The Rule of St. Benedict

7.6

Showing you care

Another important piece in the respect jigsaw puzzle is showing people that you care. The key here, however, is to make sure that you're caring about the right things. It seems that many people, particularly those striving for success, have a tendency not to do this. They care about themselves, money, winning by any means necessary and destroying the competition. However, if you care about your friends, family and colleagues; how what you do affects others; and the health of your profession, community or sector, then you will command respect and be seen to have integrity.

The great thing about caring is that if you care for others then there's every chance that they will care for you. Having people behind you who not only care about your wellbeing, but also about you becoming successful can be a powerful force pushing you towards your dream. It's also a great way of getting loyalty from your audience and stakeholders. Building a caring mentality and creating a caring culture for people can help you to overcome almost anything in the pursuit of your vision.

Some successful people have taken their levels of respect to new heights by not only showing they care about the people, parties and things that are close to them personally and professionally, but also for elements further afield, such as the disadvantaged, their community and the environment. One of the biggest displays of this kind of caring is philanthropy, which can even help to rebuild the damaged reputations of successful people – one of the most difficult of tasks.

The simple act of caring can, arguably, offer the biggest returns of any human characteristic. It immediately marks you out as a good person and will also give you great satisfaction in your success.

"Act as if what you do makes a **difference**. It does."

William James

Truly successful people care about their profession, what they do and how they affect others. Their caring cascades through four levels:

★ How you feel – Caring starts with you. You must care about your personal mission and values, and about making a difference in life. When you feel good and you care about yourself, you are up for the challenges that life brings.

★ How you make others feel – Show friends, family and work colleagues you care by taking take time to listen to their concerns, helping out with a problem or offering advice. People will remember how you made them feel and return the favour. Be aware of your impact on others!

★ How you conduct yourself professionally – Successful people care about how they go about their daily duties and how effective they are at what they do. This comes from the satisfaction that comes with having a pride in what you do, and in delivering the best for your community or customers.

★ How you support the broader community – You must extend your caring to the community you serve to ensure sustainable long-term success for all, just as the great teacher has the greater good of their school at heart, and the ambitious entrepreneur cares about the long-term viability of their sector. You can add further value by showing you care about key issues such as the environment, and charitable causes.

7.7

Patience is a virtue

Ambitious people have traditionally found patience a tough virtue to embrace. The burning desire for success often comes with an inherent internal hunger for it to happen as quickly as possible. However, the reality is that achieving your goals in life means that you will have to develop patience in order to tolerate the waiting game you face.

The frustrations associated with delay often present themselves with an agitated or upset feeling that can consume your mind. By adopting the attitude of patience, you become far more effective in controlling your emotions and impulses. This will allow you to become calm when faced with difficulties.

Needless to say, patience does not come as second nature to many of us. To help prepare yourself mentally to be more patient, you should face the fact that anything worth achieving does not happen overnight. What's more, you should open your eyes to the impression that impatience gives out to others. Displays of impatience can make you look childish, spoilt, unrealistic and desperate, and as such are unlikely to make people respect you. Patience, on the other hand, gives off a sense of calm, strength, self-confidence, control and intelligence – traits that anyone would welcome in their friend, colleague, boss, partner or client.

You can also practise the art of thinking before you speak – this starts to condition your mind to be more thoughtful and patient. By becoming patient you will enjoy the journey to success more. You'll also become more considered and take situations in your stride more readily.

The waiting game

By becoming more patient you:

★ Reduce levels of stress that lead to a **healthier** and **happier** life

★ Make better decisions, because when you are **calm** you see the bigger picture

★ Become more emotionally aware, which means you can **empathise** with people more effectively

★ This, in turn, allows you to build **wisdom**

Learning to be detached

Sometimes you have to slow down to move faster. This means you may have to make a conscious effort to just **stop** and **think**. The closer you get to a situation the more unclear it can sometimes appear, so you need to **detach** yourself from the issue. This is not easy for many of us, so you must dig deep.

"Patience and **perseverance** have a **magical** effect before which difficulties disappear and obstacles vanish."

John Quincy Adams

7.8

The art of self-control

The cornerstone of being a successful and inspirational leader is showing discipline and having the ability to control yourself at all times, no matter what the prevailing circumstances. By formulating a set of personal moral beliefs in your mind, you can avoid the unacceptable behaviours of unruliness, chaos and lawlessness that will result in disrespect and ruin your reputation and integrity.

Many successful people have gone off the rails as a direct result of not having sufficient self-discipline to curb their excesses. The world of music and media has seen many of its heroes' triumphs rapidly come to a grinding halt thanks to a lack of self-control. The inability to handle the temptations of drugs and alcohol, for example, have led many shining stars very quickly into a downward spiral that they have not been able to recover from – both in terms of their wellbeing and their popularity.

In the world of finance, a lack of ethics among its leaders produced fraudulent activities. These once respected individuals now face lengthy jail sentences and disgrace simply because of an inability to control their destructive urges.

When poor self-management prevails and human beings become intoxicated by success, it can rapidly lead to arrogance and disconnection from the real world. Many so called successful people become a law unto themselves, thinking that anything is possible. They remove the moral and ethical boundaries from their life and just do whatever they want. Unfortunately, this mindset cannot be justified.

To enjoy long-term success, you must understand where to draw the line and realise that self-discipline is a necessity. By embracing such a way of thinking, you become the author and custodian of your own rulebook for life, and someone who people look up to and respect for their strength of character.

"**Beware** of endeavouring to become a great man in a **hurry**. One such attempt in ten thousand may succeed. These are fearful odds."

Benjamin Disraeli

Maintaining discipline

Your personal conduct is governed by your acceptance of three fundamental concepts:

★ Control – You are in **charge** of your own life and you set the rules of acceptable behaviour

★ Balance – Be careful not to suffer from **burn out** and don't seek **comfort** in activities that can cause us harm

★ Grace – Handle failure with **grace** and **dignity**, then quickly move on

Remain grounded and in control. Don't let success go to your head. Stay **calm** and **centred** and never fall into the trap of thinking you are invincible. If you do, you're in for a nasty shock!

"The first and best **victory** is to conquer **self**."

Plato

7.9

What goes around comes around

You must be mindful of the actions and tactics you implement on your road to success, and ensure that they are both ethical and respectful of others. If you give out respect, then there's every chance it will come back to you.

The same applies to a number of circumstances. For example, avoid making enemies of anyone within your community – whether rivals or not. Firstly, this is not a good way to handle situations. Secondly, it's reckless and dangerous to allow someone to have a grudge against you, and it can come back to haunt you when you least expect or want it to. It's also important not to take advantage of people, so don't ask someone to carry out a task you would not undertake yourself.

Always aim to do the best you can and extend a hand of assistance to those that would benefit from your guidance. If you can spare time for others, then do so. If you can't, respectfully decline, but explain why. However, don't leave people feeling they have nowhere to turn, so offer some form of advice that can at least help someone progress.

When you extend a hand of encouragement to someone, hopefully that person will do the same for others they encounter. Your aim should be to foster a virtuous circle of support that contributes to the personal growth of ambitious people. By contributing in such a way, your intervention becomes appreciated, respected and further down the line someone will help you in your time of need.

In general life rewards those that contribute, help and display compassion to those in need. Like a boomerang, the help comes back to support you in the very same way you intended to assist others. The inspiration you require usually comes out of the blue when you least expect it!

> "Life is a **gift**, and it offers us the priviledge, opportunity, and responsibility to give something back by **becoming more**."

Anthony Robbins

Give without expectations...

When you **help** an individual, the great thing is that you're likely to get a **return** on your investment of time and support. However, it's important that you offer such help from the perspective of not expecting anything in return. Contribute because it's the **right thing to do**, not because you'll benefit yourself. You must avoid the "What's in it for me?" that has dominated society for so long. A mindset based on a servant mentality will always win in the end.

...but beware the serial takers

While it's good to offer help to people when you can, make sure your **generosity** and altruism isn't being exploited. Be wary of those that just keep taking. If you feel your offering is being abused, then its time to back off. But, again, do this with candour and explain your reasoning.

> "Like gravity, **karma** is so basic we often don't even notice it."

Sakyong Mipham

7.10

The philosophy of giving

When you become blessed with spiritual or personal wealth, embark on a mission to give to those who will benefit from your privileged position. Your contribution can be tangible, such as money, food or other material goods. However, giving can also relate to invisible yet invaluable assets, such as expertise, knowledge and experience. Ask yourself: "Would someone else benefit from what I have?"

Observing a worthwhile cause prosper from a valuable contribution you make is an extremely rewarding personal experience. It's also a powerful way of showing that you appreciate what you have and are generous and kind-hearted enough to want to spread your wealth among those less fortunate.

Carried out in the right way, acts of philanthropy can make you a highly respected figure in your community or sector, and may even open further doors of interest and opportunity, while helping you forge relationships that could be both rewarding and helpful in taking you further.

You will experience a strong sense of pride and personal worth when you make a valued contribution to a cause that supports the progression of talent. You are also like to benefit from good publicity that will enhance your reputation. However, it's vital that you only participate if you have a deep-rooted desire to make a difference. Any sense of your generosity being seen as a token gesture could seriously harm your standing. Contribute from the heart, otherwise any impact will be short lived.

You should view success as a two-way street. First you accept the fortunes that it brings and, second, you should embark on a personal mission that gives something back. By embracing this way of thinking you will benefit from a great sense of achievement and give more meaning to your life.

> "It is every man's **obligation** to put back into the world at **least** the **equivalent** of what he takes out of it."
>
> *Albert Einstein*

Supporting roles

It's **rewarding** to show that, despite your success, you have not forgotten your **roots** or people in need. So explore viable ways in which you can proactively help a segment of society. Some ideas could include:

Charity – How can you support beneficiaries through fund-raising activities or charitable **donations**?

Offer your time – How you can provide **expertise** to support new and emerging talent?

Mentor – **Commit** personal **time** to offer one-to-one support to individuals that have a vision of their own.

Sponsor – **Pledge** your support to causes that you spiritually and emotionally **connect** with and relate to.

> "No one has ever become poor by **giving**."
>
> *Anne Frank*

connection, insight, pitching, brand, impact, relationship, listening, consistency, features, benefits

Step 8

Engage with people

Everyone will have their own personal view of what success means. But whether it's being a successful entrepreneur, becoming a professor, running a successful charity, or doing something else entirely, the chances are that you'll have an audience that you need to impress. These are the people who will have a crucial influence over whether you make it or not. The more you can get their attention in the right way, the greater the chances are that they'll deliver the response you're looking for to make you successful.

The key here is not only to make effective connections, but also to do this appropriately. By combining strong communication with the right delivery method, you will maximise engagement, which is the kind of connection you're looking for, as it shows your audience that you have taken the time to find out about them and their desires, and how to reach them to the best effect.

There are key factors that determine how effectively you engage with people. This chapter will guide you through these important areas to help you communicate with your audience in the way that will gain the best response, and take you closer to your vision.

8.1

Looking through their eyes

Proactively moving towards your goals means that you will have to work hard at connecting with and influencing others to embrace your way of thinking. The quest to create win-win relationships with key partners, members of your stakeholder groups and customers or others who use your service should be a primary objective. The starting point is to be able to view things from their perspective – not only yours.

If your own personal needs are all that matters, then people will detect this and question your motives. The lack of interest in the other person's world very clearly signals that you are out just for yourself. This becomes a real danger zone for any ambitious person who wants to achieve their goals, particularly if getting people on side is a key strategy to moving forward.

When you enter into discussions with potential partners, customers or individuals that need to be influenced, your chances of a positive outcome will be greatly enhanced if you do your homework. The necessity for preparation cannot be underestimated.

The very process of getting closer to someone means that you are better informed. Your messages become well targeted and you equip yourself with a far better chance of fending off any potential challenges or opposition. Your ability to anticipate and deal with these issues will position you as both professional and credible.

Spend time looking at what is important to the people you need to influence. Once you master the art of living in the world of others, your ability to display genuine added value will become well appreciated. You will them come to excel at connecting with others, and will also learn how to fine tune your approach to add even more value to your relationship.

"The **beginning** of knowledge is the **discovery** of something we do not understand."

Frank Herbert

Getting under their skin

Try to get into the **mindset** of key people and groups by:

★ Understanding their **needs** and motivations
★ Gaining insight into issues important to them
★ Finding out more about the problems and challenges they are **experiencing**
★ Figuring out their plans and strategies for the future
★ Discovering their **expectations** of others

"**Knowledge** makes a god of me."

Anonymous

8.2

Life's a pitch

Success involves people and organisations having to sell what they have to offer – this could be your skill, a product or service. This term frightens many, as it conjures images of unethical smooth-talking individuals manipulating others to get their own way. This is not the case. A great pitch is grounded in ethical behaviour fused to a mindset of offering real value through a passionate belief in what you have to offer.

Personal and professional progression means that you will frequently be in a situation where you have to pitch for what you want. Applying for a career promotion, a place on the school board or attracting new customers fundamentally means you are in competition and there is a need to sell. If you don't adopt a selling mindset and carefully prepare your pitch, then you will struggle to get what you want out of life.

You need to embrace the pitch mentality. This isn't about becoming an archetypal salesperson or overselling. It's about distilling your offer and sharing your passion in a clear, logical, engaging and convincing manner. Simply going through this process can help to give you focus and direction. Convincing others of the benefit of your talent, idea, product or service is an integral component to achieving your goals.

Make sure that you practice your pitching skills to enhance your chances of success. It will put you in a stronger position to fend off any competition.

"If you are **not** moving **closer** to what you want in sales (or in life), you probably aren't doing enough **asking**."

Jack Canfield

When you find yourself in a situation where selling is vital, start by asking:

★ Do I understand their world?
★ What problem am I going to solve for the person I am pitching to?
★ What do I know about my audience?
★ What value do I bring?
★ What examples can I use to evidence credibility?
★ How can I bring to life the impact I make?
★ What is special about what I have to offer?

"The fact is, everyone is in **sales**. Whatever area you work in, you do have **clients** and you do **need** to **sell**."

Jay Abraham

8.3

Deliver a clear proposition

Having a clear proposition and articulating it with ruthless simplicity is a skill you must acquire. All too often key messages can get lost in the excessive use of language. The result is that, no matter how strong your offer, your communication fails to resonate with your audience. This lack of engagement could prove fatal if you don't do something to solve the problem.

Acquiring the skills to be able to deliver your proposition with impact, in an engaging way will significantly enhance your chances of getting others to listen to what you have to say. This is very important as you will often only get one chance to make a point or speak to an individual who could influence what you want to achieve.

When you embrace a mindset that allows you to project what you have to say in a concise and effective way, you engage the interest of others and your opinions are digested and taken on board. When combined with an effective understanding of the needs of others and a well-prepared pitch, the things you want to say will become much clearer and concise. As a result, they will rapidly engage the attention of others.

Effectively getting across your proposition is something you can work on and hone as time goes by, as you refine your offer and learn from experience. So always remember, practice makes perfect.

The FBIE model: Features. Benefits. Impact. Evidence.

The proposition development model of FBIE is a great way to start **developing** your skills. It allows you to package your proposition in such a way that it **captivates** the interest of others and gets them on side. The model sets out the key elements of your proposition:

★ Features – main characteristics of your offering
★ Benefits – how it improves the recipient's current situation
★ Impact – the measurable difference you can make
★ Evidence – an example of where you have done it before

"A **wise** man proportions his **belief** to the **evidence**."

David Hume

Your proposition must aim to encapsulate the:
★ **Value** you bring
★ Difference you will make
★ Problems you **solve**
★ Elements of what sets you apart from others

"Try not to become a man of success but rather try to become a **man of value**."

Albert Einstein

8.4

Building your personal brand

Beyond understanding your proposition and being impressed by your pitch, when people 'purchase' what you offer, they will also be buying into you – and to a certain extent, your vision. As this is your dream you are pursuing and, therefore, your operation to achieve it, you are likely to be the figurehead. From Virgin's Richard Branson to easyJet's Stelios, more and more organisations are using their figureheads to engage with their audiences and support their proposition and brand. In a highly competitive environment, it can help you create a key point of difference.

To do this effectively, you need to develop your own personal brand that is strongly aligned with your vision and any operation you are leading. And you need to do this very carefully and with a lot of thought as you are linking your reputation directly to that of your organisation and your offer. You also have to prepare your mindset so that you are reflecting your brand. Obviously your image must be sympathetic, relevant and attractive to your audience, as it needs to have an affinity with you, ideally both emotionally and functionally.

Ultimately, this is all about your personal chemistry. Successful people have a powerful ability to connect with others through their personality and personal power. Start to cultivate your personal brand, as the success of future relationships, partnerships and connections will largely hinge on how others view and perceive you.

Think about your own personal brand and how you are perceived. Do the best job you can, develop an ability to engage with your community effectively and be a great communicator. Also be clear on what you stand for and don't deviate from a strong ethical position. By doing this you will build a strong personal brand – one that others will want to associate with.

"Your personal brand is a **promise** to your community... a promise of **quality**, consistency, competency, and **reliability**."

Jason Hartman

You can think of your personal brand on three levels:

★ Functional mastery – The **expertise** you bring and what you are good at. This element of your personal brand should articulate that you are **accomplished** at your vocation, trade or profession. Others will trust your judgement when you know what you are talking about.

★ Social mastery – This is the ability to **communicate** effectively with others and develop meaningful dialogue. The social dimension also extends to the personal networks with which you associate. Credible, honourable and professional people tend to maintain ethical and similarly professional company – all too often you can be judged by your **alliances**, so be careful.

★ Spiritual mastery – This relates to how you **conduct** yourself, and the personal beliefs and values you hold. Strong personal **brands** deliver on their **promises**, they are extremely ethical and transparent in how they conduct themselves and their life.

"Good **reputation** is more **valuable** than **money**."

Publilius Syrus

8.5

Making an immediate impact

The art of great connectivity and engagement involves making a positive impact almost immediately. This enables you to press ahead with interacting and encouraging a constructive exchange of views that brings value to both parties. If you can do this you will become known as someone who can put people at their ease by empathising with them, and then bring the most out of them to maximise the effectiveness of a meeting for all concerned.

At a job interview, the ability to quickly make people feel comfortable helps them feel positive towards you and more receptive of what you have to say. During a presentation to a new group of customers, this will enable you to grab their attention and give you more time to explain your offer.

A number of factors determine how quickly you can personally engage with your audience. Your tone needs to be warm and inviting from the off, while you should also have an air of authority and confidence, without displaying arrogance. You also need to prove your knowledge and experience early on, while not being afraid to get your audience involved by asking their opinion or if they have any questions for you. You will also need to look the part, but this should suit your audience, rather than simply looking as smart as you can. If you overdo it, you can come across as intimidating.

Within a short time you are aiming to get people to trust you and view you as credible, while building a rapport with your audience to maximise engagement.

To the **maximise** the effectiveness of your first encounters with new people, make sure that you get the **small things** right. Failure to be conscious of some of the following may lead to creating the wrong impression:

Personal appearance – Dress in the way you want to be perceived. Your dress sense almost becomes part of your persona. Good grooming means that we take **pride** in ourselves, and it often translates into other aspects of our life. If your dress sense is incongruent with the circumstances and situation you then this will dominate the other people's thoughts.

Hospitable and welcoming – When you are accepting guests, it is vital that you are **hospitable**. The welcome you provide others demonstrates a high degree of caring and respect. A warm welcome creates a **positive climate** for a discussion and good basis for a relationship to start. An environment that fails to address basic human needs will make it hard to cultivate relationships.

Smile – The majority of individuals prefer to work and associate with **positive** people. One of the most basic ways of demonstrating is simply by **smiling**.

Be there – The next time you meet with someone make sure that you are **present!** All too often in meetings people are in a state of semi-consciousness, with their minds wandering, so that they come across as thinking about something completely unrelated. This simply shows a lack of respect.

"A **smile** is the universal **welcome**."

Max Eastman

8.6

Frame of Mind

Before any important interaction with individuals or groups of people, you must avoid launching yourself into the situation without being totally prepared. This preparation involves doing your research into the subject matter and getting into the right mindset.

First you need to ask yourself if you're totally conversant with the messages that you want to give and whether you have made the necessary preparation. It's vital that you come across as being confident and informed, as more people will believe you and listen to what you have to say. But you can only do this when you've done your homework.

Second, you must spend time mentally preparing for meetings, presentations and interactions that are important to your success. A mindset that is not focused on delivering a successful presentation or meeting will at best produce a satisfactory performance. You need to take time to tailor your thinking to the event. This means getting into the right mindset for what you're about to do.

The more you practice becoming mentally prepared, the better at it you will be. Combining this with thorough research into your subject will mean you won't need to impose any limits on what you want to achieve and will prevent fear from holding you back from making important connections. Soon you will have mastered the art of communicating effectively at different levels, from one-to-one interactions through to small and large groups. Having a firm grip on your material and then getting into the zone will help to give you the ability to engage effectively with anyone. The more you practise the more competent you become.

Getting in the zone

You can become mentally prepared for your audience by:

★ Creating a mental image of the desired outcome. Set an intention and write it down.

★ Keeping telling yourself that the outcome will be what you want. By doing this you set yourself up for success.

★ Rehearsing. Think through what you are going to say and create a mind map of all the key points you want to get across. Most importantly, think about the opening words and first few sentences.

★ Using deep shallow breathing to help calm any nerves.

★ Always creating time for solitude before an important event, meeting or interaction. This will bring order into your thinking and avoid a cluttered mind.

"If you hear a voice within you saying, 'You are not a painter', then by all means paint and that voice will be silenced."

Vincent Van Gogh

8.7

Being consistent

Your ability to maximise the engagement of your audiences relies not only on the messages you give out about your proposition and offer, or how you deliver them, but also on consistency. This has two levels that are equally important to making effective strong connections.

First, you must be consistent from a personal perspective. If you live life against the backdrop of an ongoing shift of views, opinions thoughts and promises, others will find it hard to connect with you. This is because they are never quite sure what to expect. A mindset without some degree of steadfastness will result in a situation where relationships are hard to build, and respect for your views and personal credibility become difficult to establish.

Not only that, but the image you project – your personal brand – and your moods need to be consistent and aligned to your vision. This shows people that you are reliable and helps build an all-important platform of trust. After all, if people can't believe what you say, they are unlikely to buy into your proposition and offer, and this will mean that key connections that can help you towards your goal will not be made.

Second, the message you are delivering should be consistent, as each time you present or discuss your offer you are then reinforcing your proposition. It will also help to give your audience a clearer picture and avoid any confusion.

Engagement will be greatly enhanced if you are consistent in the messages you communicate and the behaviours you display.

"Always be **consistent**."

Casey Kasum

> "More and more, I want the consistency rather than the **highs** and the **lows**."
>
> *Drew Barrymore*

How consistent are you? Review yourself across these four areas:

★ Moods – Do people find it hard to 'read' you and decide whether you are in a good or bad state of mind? Are you approachable irrespective of how you are feeling? Don't let your mood affect how you govern your day, or you will run the risk of alienating others.

★ Personal value and beliefs – Do you live the values and beliefs you promote? Or do you manipulate them to get what you want out of life? By doing this you start to live a lie and others will perceive you as being out only for yourself.

★ Goals and ambitions – When you set your goals, do you achieve them no matter the circumstances or situations you're in. When life gets hard or the goal seems unobtainable, do you move onto the next thing? This sends out very negative messages, as others will view you as lacking in tenacity.

★ Work – Is the quality of your work and professional life of a consistently high standard? Do you honour your promises to colleagues and team members, or are you seen as someone who fails to do what they ask? There should be no place for mediocrity in your life and it's vital that you are reliable and trustworthy.

8.8

Unleash your enthusiasm

Enthusiasm is a highly contagious, engaging and extremely powerful force you can use to build relationships and form new connections. It is far more pleasing to interact with individuals who are highly energised and motivated by what they do, than spend time with people who seemingly just can't be bothered.

If you suppress your feelings about the things you love to do, you run the risk of cultivating an image of apathy. It can result in others forming opinions that fail to do justice to your ability, skill and competence. Enthusiam is all about making your feelings come alive. It's the manifestation of your passion and it should be delivered confidently and clearly to those you wish to influence.

By allowing your enthusiasm to rise to the surface, you can fast track the achievement of your goals. This is because you will be making it very clear to others how much a certain issue, topic or aspect of your vocation or professional life means to you. You'll do this in such an exciting way that your energy will become infectious and galvanise others into action to support you. In this way, enthusiasm can be a strong motivational tool. It can also be a great vehicle for adding value and showing the difference you can make.

However, you need to find the dividing line between enthusiasm and coming across as over-zealous to avoid annoying your audience. The last thing you want to do is alienate others to your views. So be aware of the audience you are interacting with and mindful of their personalities. If necessary, curb you enthusiastic behaviour to suit personal preferences.

The spirit of enthusiasm clearly signals to others your zest for life. This in turn creates charisma – your personal chemistry – which is highly effective in getting your message across.

> "Enthusiasm is the mother of **effort** and without it nothing **great** was ever achieved."
>
> *Ralph Waldo Emerson*

Showing your passion

You can channel your **enthusiasm** in your dealings with others to get across your passion, **inspire** and **engage**. You can do this by:

- ★ Projecting your voice clearly and concisely articulating your thoughts.
- ★ Using open body language and gestures to show how you feel – be animated.
- ★ Having opinions, but not by being opinionated. Avoid being viewed as dictatorial or arrogant.
- ★ Using visual aids and props to make key points come alive.

> "Enthusiasm is **excitement** with **inspiration**, **motivation** and a pinch of **creativity**."
>
> *Bo Bennett*

8.9

Actively listening

Paying proper attention to what other people have to say is one of the most important life skills you need to acquire. Actively listening will have a profound impact on your personal and professional life.

By making a conscious effort to digest what others have to offer, you gain useful information on which to base decisions and knowledge to support personal progression. This means opportunities present themselves with greater clarity. Listening also demonstrates to people that you care about and appreciate their views and feelings – a vital component for building relationships based on mutual respect.

Creating an environment and a regime that allows you to have periods of calm reflection has the effect of heightening your levels of consciousness, which helps you to become a more effective listener. This means making time for regular breaks in order to take a step back from the buzz around you to clear your mind.

By freshening your mind, you create more space to absorb what's going on around you. Your mind becomes a receiver of information, which you can act upon more effectively.

This structured approach to listening enables you to construct replies that do away with shooting from the hip – you become more considered in your thinking. The fact that you have been taking everything in and building this into your reply makes you more engaging to your audience. Active listening allows you to pick up on opportunities that would have otherwise been missed as a result of the mind noise. So listen with both your eyes and ears.

Paying attention

The art of **listening** lies far deeper than merely picking up on the words that others say. It involves a heightened state of **awareness** – one that takes into account:

★ Hearing what is being said and why – the point being made and the motives behind it.

★ The need to defer judgement by reflecting on the true meaning of what is being said.

★ The body language that accompanies the words – are they congruent?

★ Assembling a response by assimilating the various points made.

★ Responding with a meaningful reply.

"When people talk, listen **completely**. Most people never listen."

Ernest Hemingway

These simple steps of listening allow you to **respond** effectively with insight and value. Conscious listening demonstrates **professionalism**. It enhances your reputation and improves the quality of your decision making.

"Make sure you have finished **speaking** before your audience has finished **listening**."

Dorothy Sarnoff

8.10

Relationships are key

Building strong relationships with your colleagues, stakeholders, partners and customers will heighten your level of engagement with them, and can play an important part in achieving your goals. Creating harmonious partnerships is also extremely satisfying, as it makes your life and work both rewarding and fun.

Great relationships don't just happen overnight, they progress and grow over time. You get more out of relationships the closer both parties get to each other. Sustainable partnerships and alliances with your stakeholder groups go through three phases:

Seed – The start of a relationship involves getting to know each other. Get the basics right and do the small things that establish fundamental trust. Securing an order with a new customer, for example, means that you deliver on time and provide a service that excels. If you have just secured a new job, be punctual, keen and enthusiastic. Show a willingness to be involved and get stuck in.

Nourish – Extend the relationship by taking greater risks. With your new customer, for example, introduce new products and services. Having settled into the new job, take on more responsibility and be proactive as this shows initiative. Demonstrate that you are committed to learning and development. Achieve the objectives that you have been set.

Flourish – Build on good will that has been created through the previous phases. Take the relationship to an advanced level by making time for activities that extend the normal working day. Share personal time within the framework and parameters of professional behaviour. Raise your bar of performance and excel – deliver the unexpected.

Relationships take time to cultivate, so don't attempt to force them along too quickly. They must take a natural course and you need to be mindful of taking anyone for granted, as it is sure to backfire!

Mutual benefits

Apply some simple ground rules to make relationships work for both parties:

★ Start with a **win-win** mentality. Each party must benefit in equal measures.

★ Have more yes's than no's – aim to accommodate each other's views.

★ Patience – it won't always go to plan, so you must be **tolerant**.

★ Be up front – if there's an issue, get it on the table.

★ Show **respect**.

"Think **win-win:** a habit of highly successful people."

Stephen Covey

Taking the time **to build** strong personal and professional **relationships** is the strongest way to **engage** with people, as they will have a personal **investment** in you.

"**Great** relationships are based on **more** yes's than no's."

Harvard University Business Review

appeal, uniqueness, intuition, authenticity, advantages, ground breaking, creative soul, stand out from the crowd

Step 9

Gain an edge

Whether you're striving to be a rock star or a successful entrepreneur, there are likely to be other people trying to take a similar route to success. These people are your rivals as they are in competition with you for the attention of your audience. As a result, their level of appeal will directly affect how quickly and successfully you realise your vision.

However, you can steal a march over your rivals by thinking carefully how you can stand out from the crowd. Shining more brightly will help you to gain a competitive edge as you'll be more visible to your audience and draw more people to you.

This is all about daring to be different, and, of course, it comes with a risk. You could play it safe and stick to what you know works, but by doing so you may never reach the heights you crave. But if you decide to plough your own furrow, there is always the chance you could alienate the people you want to attract.

This chapter explains why it's important to be innovative and strive for a key point of difference to gain an edge. It also sets out the way you can achieve this with the minimum amount of risk and develop a mindset that is constantly switched on to new ideas.

9.1

Creative thinking

To stand out in your community or marketplace and give yourself a competitive edge, you first need to think carefully and creatively about how you can differentiate yourself. You will need to create a mindset that delivers original and innovative thinking. You need to prepare yourself mentally to generate the inspiration you need. Rather than the usual flashes of inspiration and innovative ideas, you need to try to discipline yourself and train your brain to come up with them on a regular basis. This means setting aside time in your schedule to create the right environment that will be conducive to creative thought.

First, you need to take sanctuary from your busy life. Inspirational thoughts are unlikely to present themselves when you are anxious or stressed, or if you have your mind cluttered with other things. You should allocate a proportion of your time to uninterrupted thought – ideally 10 to 15 minutes a day. This will help you to work out innovative solutions to the challenges and opportunities you face. By making time for silent reflection, you will be able to focus more clearly on important issues, such as how you can add value to your offer to make it stand out and appeal to your audience.

Connecting more regularly and effectively in this way with your "creative soul" will increase your chances of success. By accessing this zone, you will solve problems more effectively, approach difficult situations more objectively, and come up with better options on how to progress. When you quieten your mind and tune into your inner voice, you will find a clarity of thought that delivers inspired focus and guidance, taking you closer to your vision.

Liberating your creative soul

Don't use the excuse that you don't have **time** for silent contemplation. Let go of being too **busy** and allow your creative soul to speak. Here are some simple steps you can take to achieve this:

★ Write down the challenge, opportunity or issue you need to resolve – be precise and specific.

★ Repeat this three times.

★ Find your place of sanctuary – no telephone, radio or noise of any kind.

★ Use slow breathing to meditate on the challenge.

★ Do this for 15 minutes, and at the end of the session write down any ideas.

The answer will come to you at the **right moment**. Practice is **vital**. You must be consistent and you must commit to this activity. No one is too busy to find 10 to 15 minutes a day. It is these moments of **planning** that will deliver a **lifetime** of **freedom**.

"It is better to have **enough** ideas for some of them to be **wrong**, than to be **always right** by having **no ideas** at all."

Edward de Bono

9.2

Discovering your uniqueness

Whatever your vision may be, you'll achieve your dream if you can differentiate yourself from others, rather than simply becoming a "me-too" player. This is because it will help you to define your own unique audience. As you will play a key part in meeting your goals, before considering the originality of your offer, you need to carefully think about how you personally are different and what you possess that others don't.

Every person has their own set of unique talents and gifts. However, many people have great difficulty in articulating or displaying what they are. But it is these nuggets that help you to build that all-important point of difference. Communicating what is special about you or what you offer is particularly pertinent in competitive situations. Standing out from the crowd is a critical driver for success and helps you to attract more attention from the people who will be crucial in helping you see through your mission. All too often, your authenticity is masked by your inability to clearly define your personal and professional proposition.

You must condition your mindset to understand what makes you unique. It is a question that at some point in your life you are likely to be asked – and your success may depend on your answer! You need to deliver a response that is powerful, engaging and passionate. When you have a clear appreciation of your authenticity, it gives you the confidence to pursue your goals and accomplish your mission in life.

Making a difference

"Personal power is the ability to take action so use it ."

Anthony Robbins

Work out your unique proposition statement by exploring:

★ What makes you unique
★ What your unique talents are
★ What makes you special
★ Why others should listen to you
★ What attributes others value
★ The successes you have already achieved
★ The impact you have had on others

Summarise in 300 words your reflections on the above. By going through this process you will gain greater insight to your personal competitive advantage. Once you have clearly defined in your mind exactly what makes you different, you'll be surprised how much more success you attract.

"The world is but a canvas to the imagination."

Henry David Thoreau

9.3

Challenging conventional wisdom

In your mission to realise your vision, you are bound to come across barriers that you need to either find a way around or overcome. Sometimes these could be certain rules or ways of thinking that prevent you from taking a particular action that would accelerate you along your journey to success. Such obstacles can be created by conventional wisdom – a term used to describe ideas or explanations that are generally accepted as true by the public or by experts in a field. However, the term also implies that the ideas or explanations, although widely held, are unexamined and, hence, may be re-evaluated upon further examination.

Many of us conduct and live our lives within the framework of these established principles of wisdom. They can govern our personal life, relationships, work and professional advancement. For many of us, they can have an overwhelming influence on the way we think and behave. This applies to both individuals and organisations. However, you must acknowledge that conventional wisdom can limit your thinking and create boundaries to your aspirations. It can misguide your intentions and infer that some things are not possible, when in reality they are.

So when conventional thinking blocks your path, it's important that you are not afraid to question it, with the aim of establishing whether it is true wisdom or simply dogmatic views on how things operate or are done. It is vital that you don't take this kind of wisdom at face value. If you do, then you may miss out on discovering whether it is right or wrong, which could hinder you in your quest to realise your vision. Proving that conventional wisdom doesn't necessarily hold true could remove a barrier that everyone else is having to overcome and so give you an edge over your competition.

"You have to **believe** in the impossible."

Howard Head

Question the experts

Successful and ambitious individuals will, if necessary, **contest** conventional **wisdom** that surrounds their circumstances. A burning desire to pursue a dream or satisfy a need that is not being catered for can lead us to **challenge** a **preconceived** ideology that masquerades as **wisdom**.

Don't take the words of experts as being that of the oracle. While their wisdom may have **value** and a role to play, it does not automatically mean they are right and that their word is final. Listen to your **instincts**. Ask yourself if what you're being told seems **right**. If it doesn't, then don't be afraid to ask questions and find an answer to your misgivings.

We can run the risk of our **creative energy** and new ideas being misdirected by people supposedly in the know. Don't think twice about challenging views. **Breaking new ground** often means "creating new wisdom".

"Swim **against** the stream that will get you **noticed**."

Tim Waterstone

9.4

Using your intuition

On your journey to fulfilment you will have to make a number of critical decisions. Your success will greatly depend on the route you choose in each case. However, there are likely to be more than two outcomes in many cases and sometimes the obvious or easiest way will also be taken by everyone else. This means it is unlikely to take you any further ahead in the race to realise your dream, particularly in relation to your competitors. Consequently, you should try to think more deeply to ensure you make the best decision for you, rather than the one that you think will be most popular or the safest.

To do this you need to tap into your unique experience and knowledge, as it is this intuition that can give you an edge in the decision making process. The effectiveness and benefits of your intuition will be maximised when you believe in yourself and know exactly what you want out of life. Successful people often talk about using their gut feelings to make important decisions. However, this is only mobilised when all rational thought has been exhausted and a final decision has to be made.

You'll make the best decisions when you have asked the right questions. Without being armed with the right information, you are unlikely to make the best judgement calls. Relying purely on your instincts and listening solely to your inner voice can be dangerous, so you should probe on both rational and intuitive levels. Assimilating all the rational evidence you can, as you should with any important decision, and then applying your intuition for further inspiration is the route to making groundbreaking judgements that can take you ahead of the field and closer to your vision.

The three key questions

Before the next big decision, ask yourself:

1. Do the facts make **sense**? This requires you to assemble all the intelligence you have on the matter in question. This involves reading and speaking to people that you **trust**.

2. Does it feel **right**? This means that the decision should connect to your personal **values**. If it does not feel right, it probably isn't.

3. Does it **sound** right? Does it resonate in the right way? Does the verbal articulation of the **decision** sound right and comfortable? If the words don't feel right again, its probably not right.

These three questions will help you to blend the very best of logical and rationale processes with an intuitive feel. You must cover each of the three questions. Failure to do so leaves the decision down to chance.

"I feel there are two people inside me - **me** and **my intuition**. If I go against her, she'll screw me every time, and if I follow her, we get along quite nicely."

Kim Basinger

9.5

Keeping your antennae switched on

It's easy to be so consumed in following your dream that you become oblivious to the world around you. However, by closing the door to your surroundings or those around you, you are blocking out a potential source of inspiration.

New possibilities can be presented when you open your mind to and tap into your environment. Ask yourself how aware you are during the day? Is your head down and are you so engrossed in what you do that it leaves no space for lateral thinking? Our creative capital can become the ultimate source of competitive advantage and accelerate us to success – it's often what differentiates the good from the great. Opening your mind to the world helps to nurture your creative spirit.

While it is impractical to spend a large portion of your day in a contemplative state in search of that groundbreaking idea, you must aim to become more conscious of where you are and what you are seeing. This could involve tapping into and contributing to the conversations and discussions of your friends, family, team, colleagues and community. You could make this more formal with brainstorming or ideas sessions with your support group or team. You should also make sure you keep abreast of news in your key subject area and the media in general.

You must keep reminding yourself of the need to be aware. Creativity occurs when two or more things come together to generate something new. By observing more and keeping your antennae switched on, the ideas you pick up settle into your subconscious. Over time, your mind starts to connect the unconnected and it delivers fantastic new possibilities that can help you leapfrog to success. This fusion of ideas helps to keep you ahead of the pack.

"The way to get **good** ideas is to get **lots** of ideas, and **throw** the bad ones away."

Linus Pauling

We can heighten our **awareness** by:

★ Listening more **intensely** to what friends, family and colleagues have to say

★ Scrutinising our physical environment more closely

★ Becoming more aware of the people we **admire**

★ Keeping abreast of current affairs

★ Letting go of preconceived ideas and withholding any **judgement**

"There ain't no **rules** around here. We're trying to **accomplish** something."

Thomas Edison

9.6

Staying fresh

To feed your creative and innovative thinking and actions to help you stay ahead of the game, it's important not to fall into the debilitating and inspiration-sapping trap of routine. Varying your schedule and constantly looking for different sources of inspiration will keep your thinking fresh and alive, so that you're more likely to create sparks of genius.

Becoming consumed in repetitive behaviour, like a mouse on a wheel, will mean you appear to be putting in a lot of effort without necessarily getting anywhere as a result. It will deliver a mindset that lacks vision, imagination and creative spirit. When you do the same things day in, day out, you establish a routine. This state of mind both inhibits and prohibits new possibilities.

You will find that the same old problems surface, and bizarrely you'll think that by doing the same thing over and over again, the results will be different. Of course, the reverse is actually the case. To avoid slipping into a crippling routine, you must be aware of your habits, ideally before they become hard-wired into your daily schedule.

The manifestation of routine is that you experience a sense of monotony, and a feeling that you are stuck in a rut. The consequences are poor self-confidence, low energy levels and loss of purpose and direction – all of which can seriously derail the successful pursuit of your goals.

If you find yourself in this situation, you need to take steps to rewire your thinking, and place the emphasis on constantly searching for stimulus – things that will disrupt habitual behaviour, strengthen your creative muscles and deliver a freshness of thought.

> "Doing the **same** thing over and over, yet expecting different results, is the definition of **insanity**."
>
> *Unknown*

Free yourself

Try these five simple practices to fuel fresh thinking:

★ Alternative perspectives – Constantly look at your challenges from **different angles**. Ask yourself: "How would my role model address the issue?"

★ Remove yourself from the daily routine – Spend one day a month doing something **completely different**.

★ Connect with nature – Take time out in the **open air** and appreciate the wonder of the countryside. Combine this with **regular exercise**, as it provides a boost to your energy levels. It also helps you to value your existence.

★ Don't pre-judge the outcome of any situation – Just **observe** and **detach** yourself from comment. By not thinking, you clear your mind.

★ Take a look – Observe what your peers do and **share experiences** with them. Wherever possible, engage with people from other cultures, religions and regions of the world.

Doing away with routine is a liberating experience. It energises us and keeps us motivated to perform at high levels.

9.7

Bringing your ideas to life

It is very exciting to talk about new ideas and concepts. However, it is vital that you don't confuse sparkling words with constructive action. Often idea debates are accompanied by an excessive amount of time spent on reviewing, assessing and analysing feasibility. The common denominator within all these sessions is no progress.

When ideas are left in the abstract for too long, they will attract scepticism from people whose support you need to move them forward. Rhetoric becomes an obvious danger, as little progress has been made towards making the idea a reality. Ideas can then become stagnant and you run the risk of your credibility being challenged. These instances will invariably attract cynical comments from your peer group, colleagues and community.

What's more, not striking while the iron is hot could result in your concept being picked up by someone else. Alternatively, by the time you eventually deliver the proof of your idea, someone may already have launched something similar, and you'll find yourself lagging behind and lose your competitive advantage.

When ideas have been screened as having solid foundations, it is vital that the concepts are brought to life to relevant stakeholders. In the interests of creating "buy in" from those that you need onside, you must, as a matter of urgency make ideas tangible and real – unfortunately words are often simply not enough.

In convincing people of the features and benefits of your new ideas, take time to consider how you can bring them to life. When you make your ideas real, their chances of being embraced are markedly increased.

"Without the playing with **fantasy** no creative work has ever yet come to birth. The debt we owe to the play of **imagination** is incalculable."

Carl Jung

Living proof

Selling new ideas means that you must aim to give **evidence** of the **impact** they could potentially have. To achieve this, you could try:

★ Devising a pilot programme
★ Building a model or prototype
★ Creating a picture or short video
★ Setting up a demonstration

On your next mission to engage others with your ideas, remember to move quickly to some form of **visible representation** of your concepts.

"Words are sometimes not enough – we must make our **ideas** come **alive**."

Sticky Wisdom (Realness)

9.8

Overcoming the fear factor

Developing and implementing new ideas that can give you an edge often means that you have to take a step into the unknown. In moving forward with your innovative idea, you run the risk of getting it wrong. The fear of your idea not working can be a very powerful force that can hinder you from realising your true potential and ultimately throw you off course on your journey to success.

There are a wide range of factors that fuel the fear to take a creative leap in the dark and inhibit the progression of your new ideas. These include losing money, rejection and humiliation. Consequently, many great ideas stay on the drawing board and prevent people from creating something that could potentially be revolutionary, groundbreaking and inspirational.

Traditional organisational cultures also fail to either embrace or promote an atmosphere of creativity. Their stale behaviours and out-moded thinking dictate that the status quo is a far safer bet. This leaves people unwilling to compromise their position as the risk of failure could jeopardise their future prospects. Unfortunately, these barriers leave people feeling unfulfilled and frustrated at not being able to release their potential.

Excelling at your chosen vocation or profession means that you must embrace a spirit of bravery and courage. The successful implementation of new ideas means you have to explore and implement options, some of which may well not work out. Embracing risk becomes an essential behaviour of any ambitious goal-orientated person.

Don't become an "if only"

To find the **courage** to galvanise yourself into action, simply ask yourself: "What are the consequences associated with not moving forward with my idea?" Then, if you are truly **focused** on your passion, it's likely that the hazard of not following through your idea, and it becoming an "if only…", will haunt you in years to come.

"Only when we are **no longer afraid** do we begin to live."

Dorothy Thompson

The art of bravery

To step beyond your **comfort zone** and expand outside your current capabilities or way of doing things requires a real sense of **bravery**. Accepting this way of thinking and applying it to your goal setting will increase your chances of success. By practicing the art of bravery, your goals will become bigger the more successful you become!

"**Courage** is doing what you're **afraid** to do. There can be no courage unless you're **scared**."

Eddie Rickenbacker

9.9

Making your ideas work

A great way to give yourself an edge over your rivals is to come up with an innovative idea and get it out to your audience as soon as you can. The fear of getting it wrong can hold you back, so that success passes you by. But one way of overcoming this inhibitor is to be confident that your idea is going to work.

As well as coming up with an innovative concept, to become a success, you also need to give equal consideration to how you are going to implement your creative thoughts and make them happen. This means that you need to give careful thought to factors that are critical to the success of your concept. While over analysis can lead to paralysis, it is good practice to evaluate ideas against a simple framework. This enables you to make a judgement call on the likely outcome, and it can give you the confidence, strength and courage to press ahead and see your idea through to reality.

All too often, creative thought and practical reality fail to go hand in hand. The key is to strike the right balance between the two, so that you have good reason to believe that your idea will be a success. Great ideas are pointless if you can't build momentum into their implementation. A good way of doing this is to develop a way of quickly assessing the practicality of your concepts. This then gives you the driving force to pursue them.

Increase your chance of winning

A simple equation will enable you to look at your **creative** ideas and assess the likelihood of a **winning** result:

Successful idea into action
=
Sense test x Who x Resource

★ Sense test – The idea must pass the sense test. This means being clear on what problem the idea is solving, the scale of the **opportunity**, who will **benefit** and **why**. You also need to establish what existing or latent **needs** will be satisfied, what value the new idea brings, how it will **improve** people's lives and what is the financial commitment and associated risk.

★ Who – Without a champion, successful implementation will be challenging. So who is going to lead on taking it **forward**? Is there a need for complementary skills? Do you have the right **team** in place to make it a success? What gaps do we need to fill in the team to take the idea forward?

★ Resources – Implementation of ideas will need the appropriate allocation of **resources**. What resources are needed over and above people and finance? Do you need further **expertise**? What additional infrastructure is needed, such as premises and specialist equipment?

★ Apply a scoring system of one to 10 to each of the three areas the next time you wish to progress an idea. If you score below in any one area, then ask yourself what you can do about it.

9.10

Making yourself memorable

Success invariably means that individuals and organisations must work hard to gain a foothold in environments where competition is fierce. For example, getting a job interview with a prestigious employer, reaching new customers, winning a place on a high-performing sports team. Once you get the break, to maintain your success and progress further, you need staying power.

The Memorable Principle is a simple creative philosophy that states that you acknowledge, notice and remember things that are outstandingly different. Continually ask yourself: "How can I be memorable?" Maintain a log of great ideas that you view as being really effective in capturing the imagination. What can you learn and use to your own advantage?

In sport, you become memorable by putting in hours and hours of practice, and reaching a level of fitness and skill that places you above the competition. In business, it's bringing a high degree of perceived value over and above other players. Maybe it's an innovative brand or advertising campaign that's carries with it the "wow" factor.

The simple things often make you memorable. This could be the level of service you offer or just caring about what you do. Delivering something of great value when the recipient was not expecting it can leave a long-lasting impression. The knock-on effect from this is that your reputation will grow in stature, helping to keep you ahead. This will also lead to more and more people finding out about the great the experience you provide, creating a snowball effect on your success.

> "Practice the Memorable Principle – the things that makes you truly **unique**."
>
> *Tony Buzan*

Staying power

You can apply the Memorable Principle on two levels: first, to get the break; and second, to maintain a long-lasting foothold to secure sustained success:

Getting the break – Often the hardest part of the success journey is getting the **opportunity**. What's in your treasure chest of ideas that will deliver a memorable experience?

Maintaining your position – You need to accept that you must continue to use the Memorable Principle to build your personal **reputation** and indeed that of the organisation you represent. By doing this you embed yourself in your community or marketplace.

> "**Change** is an attitude of **mind** and the place to start is **within** ourselves."
>
> *John Harvey Jones*

flexible, humour, performance, self improvement, options, decisive, expectations, momentum, going the extra mile

Step 10

Go the extra mile

If you're in a supermarket, and you're scanning the shelves for a particular product, you're likely to be attracted to one that offers you '10% more' for the same price. That's because you will be getting more for your money. You'll also feel better about your favourite band if they give you a 'bonus track' on their latest CD. It will probably make you feel special and like them even more. The same principle can be applied to anything you do, and can really help you in your mission to realise your vision. Finding a way to add real value to your offer is a key way to gain a competitive advantage, as well as engage more strongly with your audience and generate the loyalty, which can help to speed you along towards success.

This strategy of going the extra mile is the final success factor. In a world where many people do the bare minimum they need to, gaining a reputation for doing more than enough can help to strengthen key relationships and encourage people to stick with you. This final chapter looks at the various ways you can add value in order to not only secure the loyalty of your audience, but also provide you with a sense of pride and satisfaction in your work and, of course, take you closer to living your dream.

10.1

Doing more than enough

If you have pinned down your passion and chosen your vision well, you will be highly motivated to follow it through, enjoy the process and take pride in performing as well as you can. This should create the right environment for you to surprise and delight people by not simply doing what's required, but also overperforming and delivering extra value.

Doing more than enough will not only impress the people you're serving and make it difficult for them to go elsewhere, it will also help you build a reputation for offering great value and draw others to you. It's all about realising that through hard work and loyal commitment to your goals you may from time to time have to put in extra hours or do things that may feel punishing to either your mind or body – quite often both.

The reality is that very few people are willing to push themselves physically and emotionally to over deliver. This may involve working a weekend to complete an important project, staying late at the office to help colleagues complete a critical bid, or spending more time with a pupil struggling to grasp a learning point. By giving a little more, you become respected by your peer group and the opportunities for personal progression are enhanced, because others become engaged by your level of commitment.

You will place yourself well ahead of the competition when you do more than what was expected of you. It is also extremely rewarding both professionally and personally. Think deeply about what you want to achieve and accept that by conditioning your mind to embrace the philosophy of doing more you will become increasingly successful purely by outperforming others.

Above and beyond

Here are some key drivers that can help to instill the mindset of going the extra mile:

★ You don't want to let someone down
★ You want to **influence** a customer or stakeholder
★ You have an ambition to achieve
★ Someone needs your **help**
★ You see an opportunity others have missed
★ You see **potential** that has not been realised

"If you plan on being anything less than you are **capable** of being, you will probably be unhappy all the days of your life."

Abraham Maslow

If you can orient your mind towards giving **more,** then this mental programming becomes an integral part of your behaviour and **winning** becomes a **habit.**

"There is no traffic jam on the **extra mile.**"

Anynoymous

10.2

Training with the best

If you're going to put in the additional effort of going the extra mile for people, you need to make sure that what you do is of a high standard. Giving more mediocrity doesn't really work. You have to make sure that the extra value you're adding is definitely worth having.

So if you want to excel in your professional life, work with those people that will take you to new limits. Training with these individuals will extend your comfort zone, teach you new skills and, more importantly, allow you to gain insight to how they think. Defining who you believe to be the best in your field of work provides a benchmark for raising your own performance. Do away with any feeing of personal pride or sense of undermining your own capability, and explore how you can spend time with those you identify as best in class.

High performing organisations consciously create conditions that get their best performers to push each other to new levels of performance. If you want to achieve greater success, then align yourself to those that consistently outperform the rest. Be open in your approach to these people and politely ask for their help or advice. By asking in this way, you are delivering a compliment and acknowledging their expertise and achievement mindset. More often than not, people will help.

By training with the best you set intentions and expectations that lift your mindset to new levels of attainment. Individuals you train with are different to mentors – they are the sparring partners that you work with to develop and grow your skills on a real-time basis.

Star qualities

When you approach top performers for help and advice, the aim should be to:

★ Shadow them on meetings and in their day to day activities
★ Ask for some time to share their thoughts on why they constantly outperform others
★ Seek insight on how they think and what drives them
★ Ask them what motivates them

"We are what we **repeatedly** do; **excellence**, then, is not an **act** but a **habit**."

Aristotle

Be honourable about your intentions and by no means use the experience to gain insights that would be of disservice to them. Be clear and up front. If a conflict of interest presents itself, then walk away.

"To achieve **great** things we must live as though we are never going to die."

Luc de Clapiers Vauvenargues

10.3

Self-improvement

Personal development is the ultimate source of competitive advantage. When you stop learning, you run the risk of your career becoming stagnant. Life is one continuous learning journey and every new experience presents itself as an opportunity to acquire more knowledge. High achievers are life-time learners, combining both formal and informal means of absorbing new information. As you progress along your journey to success, you will get where you want to be more quickly if you have a strategy for learning, and a personal growth plan.

By constantly reviewing your performance, knowledge and experience, and aiming for self-improvement, you are maximising your chances of outperforming others. Your commitment to getting better at what you do will also impress people and make them confident that they are getting the best possible service. Your support group or team will also be motivated to improve themselves by the example you are setting.

To be able to improve yourself, you need to be open and honest about your current abilities and how they could be improved to help you realise your vision. It's also worth asking others for their honest opinions, as they may be able to see something that you can't. So speak openly to friends, colleagues and family to find out how they think you can improve. They will be impressed by your self-effacing behaviour and probably be only too happy to help. Commit to constant learning and you will achieve your goals more effectively.

"Give us the **tools** and we will finish the job."

Winston Churchill

"Enough of **talking it** is now time to **do**."

Tony Blair

Minding the gaps

To access the areas you need to develop further, rate yourself out of 10 in each of the following areas:

1. I have clear goals, they are pursued with a passion
2. I am resilient and deal effectively with setbacks
3. I take ownership of my professional and personal development
4. I am motivated and just get on with it
5. I am a strong and effective leader
6. I work well with others
7. I am innovative and take a creative approach to life and work
8. I am a respected individual
9. I am an effective connector and communicator
10. I always aim to excel at what I do

By answering these questions honestly, you start to build a view of what areas of your life and approach need attention. Drill down into the specifics of each of your answers and define clearly what you are going to do to improve. Then identify the resources that you will need to move you forward.

10.4

Reinventing yourself

To maintain a high level of purpose, motivation and performance so you can keep pushing the boundaries and deliver more, at some point you are likely to need to make key changes to the way you operate. It may be that you have become stuck in a routine that you need to break out of because it is halting your progress. Or your market may have changed and to keep moving forward you need to tap into a new audience, or take a different approach. Perhaps you need to relocate or expand overseas to capitalise on shifting demand or to increase success. All these initiatives require you to reinvent yourself to some degree.

You must accept that you have far greater control over your life than you realise – who you are, what you want and what you think. Your mental outlook on life, as well as your character and personality remain under your own leadership and guidance. When things don't go to plan or you feel that you are stalling in your career or personal life, its time to do something different.

You should be prepared for this and have the right mindset to be able to embrace change when necessary. When you lose motivation or the results aren't coming through, that's the time to act. You can't excel if the goalposts have moved and you are no longer aligned to your goals. To go the extra mile, you must understand the need to adapt.

Time to change

The process of reinvention means that you need to critically appraise the status quo – to look at your life or career from different angles:

★ **Why are you stale?** Why are things not working or going to plan? Are you feeling **fulfilled** and **happy** with what you have and what you are achieving? Ask others for feedback on you and your performance. Open up your surroundings.

★ **Where do you want the new you to be?** Get back to reviewing your goals. Are they clear and precise or are they lacking definition and clarity?

★ **List the key transition points.** Define what specific things need to change. Draw up an action list. Detail the new partnerships and relationships that are needed to move things forward. Draw up the new tactics and work out the vital things that will deliver a different result.

★ **Act out the changes.** Make a conscious effort to implement the changes that you need to make the transition to what you want to become. Without action nothing will happen. Make sure you signal the changes to your stakeholder group.

"When the wind of **change** blows – some build walls, others build windmills."

Anonymous

10.5

Being flexible

In your quest to give more, and so shorten your journey to realising your vision, you can gain more from being open to other ways of approaching problems or performing tasks. Offering people a number of options, doing what you can to accommodate others' requirements and being prepared to change your way of thinking or working in response to circumstances will give the impression that you are doing your utmost to deliver the best service.

Building this level of flexibility into what you do can lead to big improvements in a number of areas that are key to your success, such as your reputation and credibility, and forging strong relationships with people that matter. Individuals that consider their way to be the only way can be extremely difficult to work with on both a professional and personal level. Going the extra mile will frequently require you to display alternative ways of working, ones that do away with a single-minded viewpoint. Your mindset should accommodate different perspectives to achieve the desired outcome.

You will be valued for your flexibility, because it will show that you are prepared to be open and listen to others in order to understand their viewpoint, and then work with them to achieve mutual satisfaction. If it is your intention to lead or win over the views of others, you must be flexible in your thinking, attitude and work style – even if, in some instances, this may feel uncomfortable.

As you progress through your life and career, you will come across many different personalities. Success means that you may have to adapt your approach to suit the situation. Be conscious of the way in which you interact with others – do you dismiss views too easily or do you embrace them? Even if you do not agree with people, frankness and openness with a respectful reason will demonstrate that you have an appreciation of their position and, therefore, a flexible mindset.

> "Stay **committed** to your decisions, but stay **flexible** in your **approach**."
>
> *Tom Robbins*

Don't be a 'yes' person

Flexibility is an important element of an engaging personality. It involves being reasonable with an ability to bend your thinking. However, you should not take this too far by **compromising** your personal values, self-control or composure. If you do this, you can be perceived as weak and will lose the respect of those around you. Do not subject yourself to the whims of others as this projects the image of being a 'yes' person. When you are flexible, you are able to take **prompt action** in acquiring opportunities. The openness of this mindset also attracts others to you, because constantly saying no can be off-putting and close doors that could otherwise be opened.

> "Be **firm** on principle but **flexible** on method."
>
> *Zig Ziglar*

10.6

Being decisive

Your success is not only highly dependent on the decisions that you make, but also the speed and clarity with which you make them. Delaying making a decision can start to create a mental bottleneck, which can lead to confusion and a deep feeling of being overwhelmed. You must clear this blockage by being decisive, or your self-confidence can be undermined. This will make it more difficult to make further decisions, and your performance will suffer.

By acting quickly and firmly, you become liberated and far more gets achieved. Plus others will be impressed by your strength of character and courage. You may well be tempted to delay making a decision because you feel that you would be able to make a better judgement at some point further down the line. While this may have some merit, you must avoid procrastination as this can halt performance, have a negative effect on colleagues and dilute your effectiveness.

Balance must be achieved as some decisions do need more time and careful consideration than others. For example, beginning a new job or becoming self-employed can have massive impact on your life for years to come. When choosing a career or vocation or, indeed, trying to progress one you already have, your decisions must be made in line with the goals that you have set. This means you cannot become a successful athlete if you decide to train only once a week or become an accomplished medic without deciding to commit to ongoing learning. Making good decisions involves self-discipline, focused attention and clear thinking.

> "Pursue **one** great decisive **aim** with **force** and **determination**."

Karl Von Clausewitz

Staying detached

Quite often, making the right decision requires you to be **emotionally detached** from the situation. Under certain circumstances, your feelings can take over, resulting in you making a **subjective** rather than **objective** decision. This can be a major mistake that can affect the success of you and everyone else involved, and should be avoided at all costs. For example, it can be very difficult to reprimand an under-performing individual when you also regard them as a friend. In this instance, you need to think clearly about the **approach** you take and put yourself in the position of the other person. In such cases, **candour** can be an extremely powerful tool. If you feel too close to a situation to make an objective decision, then bring in other key people to help. This does not show weakness, but **self-awareness** and a desire to do the right thing.

> "The cure for most obstacles is, be **decisive**."

George Weinberg

10.7

Embracing pressure

Going the extra mile often requires you to be able to cope in a high-pressure environment. If you want to truly excel and be the best at what you do, you need to get comfortable with stressful situations. If you can't, you will crumble under the stresses and strains of the situation. Staying cool when everything around you seems to be falling apart is a truly admirable trait. When things are not going to plan and every implemented action seems to go wrong, it is vital to remain cool, calm and collected.

Some individuals cope better in stressful situations than others. To realise your vision, it's likely that you will need to embrace pressure and thrive on it. Handling pressure in the right way and bending it to your advantage can boost performance levels and help you go the extra mile. Furthermore, dealing with situations that others are afraid to face up to is a powerful motivator, while others will be impressed by your ability to perform under pressure.

To be a high performer, you need to show that you can stretch yourself to the limit to prove you can achieve the goal you have set. You should respond to people's scepticism in your ability to complete a difficult and stressful task by thriving in adversity and being even more determined to succeed.

The secret to staying in control is to create a mindset that lets you rise above the situation so you can put it into perspective. As the tension builds and your mind starts racing, take a break to give yourself the space to think clearly and rationally, so you can click into the next gear and decide on the right course of action. This could be bringing in more resources, changing strategy or moving deadlines forward to give yourself more time. Then you can set about carrying out the task with renewed vigour and confidence.

Pushing the boundaries

When you **commit** to ongoing **self-improvement**, continuously extend your comfort zones and create new goals, you constantly extend the **boundaries** of what you can cope with. By constantly pushing yourself to achieve more, you will find yourself in unfamiliar territory both **mentally** and physically. This new ground exposes you to new and different pressures and challenges that you will have to cope with.

"The **only** pressure I'm under is the pressure I've put on **myself**."

Mark Messier

Keep **pushing** yourself to the next level. In doing so, you will become more and more **comfortable** with the pressures these situations bring. Dealing with stress simply becomes an occupational hazard, while loving the pressure becomes a **state of mind**.

"No **pressure**, no **diamonds**."

Mary Case

10.8

Gaining momentum fast

In the same way that taking time out to think about the key issues can prove vital to controlling and thriving on high-pressure situations, so the calm-before-the-storm approach works when planning a swift assault on a key opportunity.

You will often find that you are presented with situations in life where a window of opportunity presents itself. However, they can be transient in their nature, and this means that if you don't act fast, you run the risk of losing out altogether. This process of pouncing with a sense of urgency needs a moment of calm before you mobilise the effort and build momentum very quickly.

Rushing into a situation without thinking about it can lead to disaster. Just because the opportunity may be fleeting, doesn't mean you have to be impetuous. Such an approach smacks of recklessness. If your mission fails, you'll at least have wasted a lot of time and effort. At worst, you could wreck your chances of achieving your vision and blow a hole in your reputation to boot.

When confronted with a situation where a serious opportunity exists, it's important to assess its viability. This requires a moment of calm reflection, where you can weigh up the pros and cons, as well as plan your strategy to grab the opportunity as quickly as possible. Then you can press ahead and put your plan into action with speed and precision, confident in the knowledge that the extra effort is worth it as you are pursuing an opportunity that really is too good to miss out on.

Using the RILM Framework

Before diving headlong at a potential opportunity, look at these key issues, then act swiftly and decisively:

1. Risk Scan the environment within which the **opportunity** has presented itself. What happens if it goes wrong? What are the dangers? Who else could take advantage of it and what would the implications of that be? What resources do you need and can you afford it?

2. Impact What would the impact of getting it right be and how would it **accelerate** your personal or professional ambitions? Can you afford not to take advantage?

3. Listen What does your **intuition** tell you? Does the opportunity align with your personal and professional values or does it compromise them? If it cuts across your core **beliefs**, it is probably not the right thing to do.

4. Move If you feel comfortable with points 1, 2 and 3, then swing into **action** quickly and make it happen. Don't be half-hearted, but proceed with **direction, focus** and **drive**.

"Seize the day! (Carpe diem)."

Robin Williams in **Dead Poets Society**

10.9

Being confident

If you're not happy with who you are, what you're capable of and where you're going, you will lack the confidence to make things happen and will fail in your pursuit of success. However, prepare yourself properly, both mentally and physically, to follow your passion and realise your dream, and your self-confidence will come.

Confidence is a key element to going the extra mile. When you are brimming with confidence you feel that you can take on the world. However, it's important that you're careful not to allow your self-confidence to spill over and become arrogance. To avoid this situation arising, always underpin your outward facing high energy with humility.

Confidence can be viewed in the context of three elements – your personality and mental wellbeing, your appearance and your abilities. If you lack confidence in any of these areas, then you will be off balance and will not be able to perform to the maximum. Communication with others, whether in a one-to-one situation or a group, becomes easier when you are confident in yourself and in your abilities.

When any element is out of sync, you end up with an uncomfortable feeling that manifests itself into lack of confidence. When these three areas are aligned, however, you become totally at ease with who you are and you reach a state of being where you're confident in your own skin. When you have achieved this, you will connect more effectively with others. You'll also be ready to take on new challenges and have a far greater chance of seeing them through successfully.

> "Nobody can make you feel inferior without your consent."
>
> *Eleanor Roosevelt*

The three states of confidence

If you have mastered the three states of **confidence**, then you will be perfectly positioned to perform to the maximum and pursue your dream:

★ Inner confidence (mental wellbeing) – Your direction in life is **clear** and you are **comfortable** with the path you are following. By setting these goals and moving towards them, you will achieve a clear sense of **purpose** that makes getting out of bed a pleasure. When you have a real meaning to your existence, you feel energised and motivated to get on with things.

★ Outer confidence (appearance) – Physical wellbeing and feeling comfortable with your appearance does away with any **inhibitions** that you may have about yourself. If you feel overweight or unfit, then this can have a negative impact on your confidence. Take time for regular exercise: this is both mentally and physically **stimulating**.

★ Professional confidence (abilities) – Being the master of your trade, career, vocation or profession makes you **confident** when you interact with others. When you know your stuff and are well prepared with your **knowledge** and **expertise**, you do away with nerves associated with a lack of understanding.

> "It took me a long time not to judge myself through someone else's eyes."
>
> *Sally Field*

10.10

Having a sense of humour

Although this may seem a strange subject on which to end this guide to cultivating the Success Factor, having a good sense of humour is arguably one of the most important traits you can possess. It will help to create that all-important upbeat atmosphere for those around you, helping you get the most from your people – in fact it will also act as a people magnet. Additionally, it will improve your ability to connect and engage with people, while helping to guard against arrogance by being able to laugh at yourself. What's more, it will increase your popularity, and when the going gets really tough it can help have a calming influence and help relieve the tension.

The key is to make sure that in your quest for your vision, you don't lose your sense of humour, as it is one of your key assets. If you're following your passion, you should enjoy the journey, no matter how hard it sometimes gets. As soon as you lose your ability to laugh at yourself or make light of a situation, you need to question whether you have been pulled off course, and check that you're still aiming to achieve something you love.

When you work in an environment where a sense of humour overarches the culture, you will be far more likely to be creative, innovative and productive. In controlled measures, a sense of humour can be an extremely motivating force that gets the best out of individuals and teams. Humour and laughter are the most undervalued and underrated tools in society.

Of course, humour should be used tastefully and appropriately. But it is certainly a great way to drive people to go the extra mile.

"If it's not fun, you're not doing it right."

Bob Basso

The funny side

Used appropriately, humour can reveal a lot of positive attributes that are essential to becoming a success, including:

★ Humility – Using humour in a self-deprecating way can fend off any hint of arrogance.

★ Confidence – Being able to make people laugh in meetings or during presentations shows confidence in your ability.

★ Approachablity – Humour can help to demystify you. No matter how successful you are humour can prevent you from appearing intimidating and make you more accessible.

★ An ability to engage – Making people smile can be a great way of getting them to listen, and creates a key element of variety for presentations.

★ A sense of fun – People who create fun environments will always attract people to work with them, while an upbeat atmosphere is the most productive.

★ Communication skills – Humour can be a great way of getting your message across.

★ A multi-faceted personality – Being funny shows people that there's more to you than simply pursuing your vision.

★ Creativity – Making people laugh shows quickness of thought and creativity.

"You can increase your brainpower three to five fold simply by laughing and having fun before working on a problem."

Doug Hall

This edition first published in Great Britain 2010 by
Crimson Publishing, a division of Crimson Business Ltd
Westminster House
Kew Road
Richmond
Surrey
TW9 2ND

A catalogue record for this book is available from the British Library.

ISBN 978 1 85458 5509

Printed and bound by Lesoprint SpA, Trento